Volume 3 _____ BROOKLYN

06
Masthead

07
Editor's Letter

138
Locations

08
Brooklyn From Above
Daniela Velasco

10
Nathan's Famous
Alexandra Svokos

18
Amarcord
Rebecca Bratburd

26
Roberta's / Blanca
Carlo Mirarchi

34
On the Side
Giuseppe Lacorazza

40
Diner
Andrew Tarlow

50
An Afternoon at Gloria's
Angela Almeida and John Surico

54
The Soda Fountain
Blair Pfander

58
L'Chayim: The Life of Delis
Jonathan Shipley

64
Field 5
Elena Sheppard

68
Pok Pok
Andy Ricker

78
All the Groceries Stores I've Known
Kyle Chayka

80
Okonomi
JT Vuong and Luke Davin

86
Brooklyn's Spirit
Andrew Scheinman

90
Tørst
Jeppe Jarnit-Bjergsø

94
Finally Brooklyn Fare
Matt Mark

98
Brooklyn Generic
Kyle Chayka

104
Semilla
José Ramírez-Ruiz and Pam Yung

126
Meyers Bageri
Claus Meyer

132
My Chinatown
Clare Mao

ADAM GOLDBERG
Editor in Chief

DANIELA VELASCO
Creative Director

ELYSSA GOLDBERG
Executive Editor

BONJWING LEE
Copy Editor

-

CONTRIBUTORS
Alexandra Svokos
Andrew Scheinman
Angela Almeida
Blair Pfander
Clare Mao
Christiann Koepke
Elena Sheppard
Emily Hirsch
Erick Steinberg
Giuseppe Lacorazza
Jonathan Shipley
John Surico
Kyle Chayka
Maggie Spicer
Matt Mark
Rebecca Bratburd

WELCOME

I grew up in New York, listening to my parents tell me about the old Brooklyn they knew: rides on Coney Island's Cyclone followed by hot dogs at Nathan's, late-night cheesecakes at Junior's in Flatbush, porterhouse steaks at Peter Luger, and slices of Sicilian-style pies.

While many of the places my parents spoke of still exist, the food they described is at odds with the Brooklyn I grew up with. Brooklyn as I knew it was where creative chefs went when the costs of opening a restaurant in Manhattan were too much to bear. It was where chefs driven to outer boroughs with their tweezers, fresh-milled flour, heritage farmers, and locally made pickles openly took more risks.

The tension between those two Brooklyns is what drew us to the borough for this issue of *Ambrosia*, and determining how they fit together has made this our most challenging issue to date. Because, the truth is, Brooklyn is many things to many different people. It is home to some of the most diverse neighborhoods in the country, from the Russian communities in Brighton Beach to Mexican expats in Sunset Park. It's where Michelin-starred restaurants got their starts next to old-school red sauce joints, both now part of the Brooklyn brand and exported around the world.

We selected a wrinkly, smoked chub mackerel as the cover image to represent this issue. Throughout a century of change, this assertive, smoked Atlantic fish has been on menus in Jewish delis in the 1900s and now finds a home (at a much higher price) on modern Japanese kaiseki restaurants in the borough. The cuisine of Brooklyn is simple, striking, confounding, and resourceful; in some crazy way, in this crazy borough, this fish represents all of that.

Through interviews, stories, and recipes, *Ambrosia,* Volume 3: Brooklyn explores what it is like to cook and eat in Brooklyn right now.

Regards,
ADAM GOLDBERG
Editor in Chief

Nathan's Famous
By Alexandra Svokos

It's the Fourth of July and the 100th anniversary of Nathan's Famous' hot dogs, and it's sweltering. We feel the heat on the long subway ride on the N/Q trains out to the farthest reaches of Brooklyn, just before hitting the shore. We see Coney Island when the subway goes above ground and the cars flood with sunlight. We pass blocks of apartments, a sign of the changing landscape of the borough, and then, like a mirage, a roller coaster appears.

Coney Island has to be the brightest place in all of Brooklyn. No concrete sidewalks or highrises with black glass that hobble into the grey sky. Not even the most magnificent #nofilter sunset photos on Instagram can capture the colors here. Couples on first dates and groups fumbling to sustain conversation stop their charades when they see it. In a borough full of people acting too cool to be fazed, we can't help but drop the pretense when we arrive. We're out of our seats, noses pressed to the dirty subway windows, pointing and smiling—wild again, beguiled again.

The train makes its final stop at Coney Island and off we go, giggling on the walk down to street level. We made it to the annual Nathan's Hot Dog Eating Contest. We crowd around the back of Nathan's Famous at the corner of Surf and Stillwell Avenues, penned in behind metal fences and smiling cops. There's a stage set up specifically for this bonanza underneath a giant sign with a digital clock counting down the seconds until the next hot dog eating contest. There are only two more hours left until the men's contest starts at noon.

There are people wearing felt Nathan's hot dog hats on their heads shaped just like Nathan's hot dogs. There are people holding signs for Joey Chestnut, a former champion and the clear crowd favorite.

For those not wearing a hot dog hat, the dress code is clear: Just wear something vaguely patriotic and you'll fit right in. T-shirts bearing slogans such as "Back To Back World War Champions," "Make America Great Again," "Don't Tread On Me," "'Murica" fill the crowd. Outfits stamped with images of Abraham Lincoln wearing a flag bandana, bald eagles, military men, and stars and stripes do too. Fans in t-shirts and shorts stand next to those in seersucker suits. No one minds what you wear as long as you're sporting red, white and blue from your hat to your shoes.

We are a country of overlapping irony and earnestness. You're American, but you're also likely an amalgam of the identities of your ancestors. You can thrive in the power this nation has while at the same time recognize the horrors that the same power has created abroad. You can be wildly patriotic, but with extreme reservations. You can make jokes about "'Murica" but weep when a well-timed "God Bless America" brings an attacked city together.

That line between irony and earnestness is almost completely lost on the crowd watching men hoover Nathan's hot dogs on Independence Day, where "U-S-A" chants break out spontaneously. Is this peak America or America's peak?

Crowds and ESPN cameras gather on Coney Island each year for the annual Nathan's Hot Dog Eating Competition to watch men and women, who qualify in competitions around the country, eat as many hot dogs as they can in ten minutes. Nathan's Famous has hosted this competition since the 1970s, selling it on the idea of American tradition.

In many ways, the American tradition Nathan's lays claim to is emblematic of success through capitalism and hype. In 1916, Polish immigrant Nathan Handwerker started selling hot dogs for a nickel–cents less than his competitors– and, according to tale, staged people in white coats to eat at his stand, making it look like doctors from a nearby hospital endorsed the health of his product. Through his dedication, he got himself a chain and a fortune.

Now, we're all gathered to celebrate the deeply unhealthy shoveling of what may be the most singularly American food: the hot dog, a mushed up sausage of countless ingredients. That said, the hot

dogs at Nathan's are famous for a reason. While other dogs require toppings to add flavor or cover dryness, the Nathan's hot dog stands up completely on its own. Even when it's 100 degrees outside, true salvation looks something like shuttling a burning hot slab of Nathan's Famous meat into your mouth.

"I just like the crunch of the hot dog," Pat Albergo, 58, says while standing in the crowd for the contest. Albergo grew up in Queens, but this was his first time at the contest. His father-in-law lives in Brooklyn, where his wife grew up, and the family came down for his 80th birthday. Mid-bite, he adds, "Somehow they make the hot dogs where the skin is crunchy. I don't know how they do that."

At the main event today what matters is quantity, not quality. The women's contest comes first, beginning just before noon. Richard Shea, president of Major League Eating –the 20-year-old organization that organizes competitive eating contests nationwide—is the excessively hyperbolic host of the proceedings. He introduces the competitors, focusing on reigning champion Miki Sudo and Sonya "The Black Widow" Thomas.

"The Black Widow" is so-called because she regularly beats men larger than her in competition, a character that she plays up with scowls to the crowd. "She wants to kill the men around her," Shea says of Thomas.

Sudo, 30, has a waist significantly smaller than that of the average American size-16 woman and wears her bleach-blonde hair in a high ponytail. While competing, Shea tells us to look out for "the angry pony," which is apparently code for what happens when she whips her hair back to swallow a hot dog. That, he says, is how we'll know she's on a roll. She wins handily with 38.5 hot dogs in 10 minutes.

But the men's competition is the main event. In an event about excess, male pro eaters deservedly get more attention— mostly because they can eat more than the female competitors. Between the events, Shea keeps us hyped with a series of performances. A Brooklyn ballet troupe dances to what sounds like Muzak. Eric "Badlands" Booker, a competitor, raps. All the while, two men in a fenced-in pen sandwiched between two halves of the audience flip on a trampoline.

We mill about in the crowd, pushing forward for better views of the action. Some fans step out to get their own hot dogs, appetites piqued from watching the women scarf them down. Others leave the crowd just to get a break from the unrelenting sunlight. Maryann is waiting with her four kids under an umbrella for her husband to come back with dogs for everyone.

"My husband's a big hot dog eating contest fanatic. He always watches it [on TV]. We always say we're going to go, but we never did. Now that the kids are a bit bigger, we decided to come," she says. At this point, though, she's not sure the kids will make it through the men's event. They'll probably leave and watch it at home, though her husband might stick around to see the glory firsthand.

"I just came along for the ride," she says.

Finally, the men's competition begins. 2015 was a rough year for Joey Chestnut, the most famous eater. He proposed to his girlfriend at the 2014 Nathan's competition, but they broke up just before the wedding in 2015. Newcomer Matt Stonie then had a surprise win over Chestnut. Joey "Jaws" is back to reclaim his title. Shea skimps on none of this drama in his introduction.

"He was broken and beaten and alone," Shea says about Chestnut after the 2015 loss. He was "standing like a boy without friends on the playground," until he remembered he was Joey Chestnut, a champion. "We are watching the triumph of human spirit," Shea says as the 10-minute countdown starts up and hot dogs fly down Chestnut's throat. Ten minutes later, Joey Chestnut has won with 70 hot dogs.

"He is American exceptionalism. He is America itself," Shea announces of our victor, playing loose with facts.

We learn that hype is what matters most at this competition. The contest started in the early 1970s, and press agent Mortimer Matz boastfully admitted to the New York Times in 2010 that he invented a history of eating contests to publicize the event. "We said this was an annual tradition since 1916. In Coney Island pitchman style, we made it up," Matz said. Handwerker set a 12-minute time limit to the competition to save lost money on eaten dogs.

Any store that adds a "famous" to its name is looking for longevity in customers and profits. Nathan's makes a phenomenal hot dog, but the annual contest is publicity worthy of Coney Island's trademark bright lights and flair. Yet, somehow, it's become a semi-ironic tribute to the American spirit, a Fourth of July tradition. Perhaps it's the ability to transform eating the humble hot dog into a spectacle worth cheering on—even in the blistering heat—that captures the true essence of the American spirit.

We clear out and crews begin sweeping up the confetti and refuse. We notice our horrifically sunburnt shoulders. The giant digital clock flicks, showing the countdown to the next annual Nathan's Hot Dog Eating Contest in 364 days, 23 hours, and 59 minutes.

Amarcord
By Rebecca Bratburd
Photography by Heidi's Bridge

Brooklyn is nothing if not a cluster of neighborhoods enriched by the diversity of its residents, and few communities have come to represent the borough as strongly as the Italians. Hollywood has idealized children lapping Italian ices on hot summer days, and mustachioed waiters serving mafiosos who linger at red sauce joints. While most of these images lean fictional, the food is no lie at these Italian food institutions, old and new.

Totonno's

On a hot summer afternoon on Coney Island, most of the tables at Totonno's are full even though the lunch rush is long over. Lawrence Ciminieri, whose great-grandfather opened Totonno's 92 years ago, works the coal-fired brick oven while wearing a backwards baseball cap and a Derek Jeter tee. He's taking pizzas out of the oven and chatting up customers with a loud, bass-heavy voice and assured swagger. I ask him: How has Totonno's been able to stay open for so long serving only pizza? He responds in a heavy Brooklyn (read: Italian-American) accent, "It's good, you'll see." The pizza's crust is pliable, soft, and delicately charred. The sauce, stewed from sun-kissed, vine-ripened tomatoes, lacks the excessive sweetness of what you'd find on lesser pies at a place such as Sbarro. I ask our waitress, Cookie, whose thick fringe frames her face, what makes this pizza better than the rest: "It's a secret. It's from Italy," she says, assured. It's hard to say who might take over once Ciminieri, now in his 60s, retires. His only daughter is studying to become a doctor. A doctor of pizza, we hope, for the sake of hungry patrons who wait on lines that snake around the block on summer weekends.

L&B Spumoni Gardens

Just a mile and a half north of Totonno's, in the Gravesend section of Brooklyn, L&B Spumoni Gardens sees similarly long lines in front of its walk-up pizza window, where customers can choose between square Sicilian slices, round Neapolitan pizzas, or both. At the next window, customers can order ice cream or the homemade Spumoni, a swirl of bright green dotted with pistachios, that interrupts silky layers of vanilla and chocolate ice cream. A sit-down dining room that's been known to serve an over-the-top tasting menu of all of the above is inside. I came for the square slice, arguably the biggest draw for customers. Its thick, doughy crust is generously painted with tomato sauce (maybe too much of a good thing) and a thin layer of pecorino Romano cheese speckled on top. In June, Louis Barbati, the owner and grandson of the Italian immigrant who opened the shop in 1939, was killed at his home in Dyker Heights after leaving the restaurant. There was chatter about a botched robbery and possible mafia connections. He was, apparently, wearing flashy jewelry, carrying $10,000 in cash (and a loaf of bread), and involved with an ongoing dispute with another pizza joint in Staten Island over a copycat pizza sauce. A pizza by any other hand would not be L&B Spumoni Gardens.

Lucali

The purportedly nefarious underbelly linked to pizza and Italian joints can be seen in Lucali's archives, too. Owner and chef Mark Iacono made headlines a few years ago for being involved in a knife fight. That doesn't stop celebrities—from Jay Z and Beyonce to Alice Waters—from piling into the no-reservations, BYOB joint in the famously Italian neighborhood of Carroll Gardens. Iacono uses a brick oven to mold thin crust doused in his signature sauce. But it's the cozy ambiance—chalkboard menu; dim, yellow lighting—that makes it a neighborhood favorite among regulars.

Bamonte's

Bamonte's, which is rumored to be a long-lost mob hangout, has served traditional, red-sauce Italian-American fare since 1903, and it's still run by the Bamonte family. More than a few waiters have been serving at Bamonte's for over 40 years. They all wear tuxedos, and wait on tables covered with white tablecloths, a rare dining experience to have in the casual Brooklyn of 2016. Nothing, from the decorative cigarette vending machine and the two wooden phone booths, to an antique cash register, looks like it's been updated since the 1950s. "I came here when I was ten years old!" a customer in her ninth decade told me, as she and a group of ladies carried on after lunch. Christopher, our soft-spoken and formally dressed bartender, poured a sip's worth of Sambuca in my after-lunch espresso, a long-held tradition at Bamonte's. After an hour of chatting, Christopher shook my hand sincerely to say goodbye for the day.

Faro

Out in Bushwick, Kevin Adey is the Italian-American chef and owner of Faro, an upscale Italian restaurant that opened in 2015. He makes fresh, handmade pasta every day. He says his cooking would be unrecognizable if he were to serve it in his grandmother's house. "Several pastas on the menu—gnocchi alla Romana, cecamariti, frascatelli—are traditional but they are far removed from what people think is served at a traditional Brooklyn Italian restaurant," Adey says. "Italian food is having a golden moment in Brooklyn right now. All over the borough you can find the old schoolers and the new kids like me doing some really old stuff in a very new way. L&B Spumoni Gardens, DeStefano's, Di Fara, Grimaldi's, and Roberta's are still killing it. I just hope that in 30 years someone will say that about Faro."

Emmy Squared

Grimaldi's

Emmy Squared

Faro

Faro

Emmy Squared

Carlo Mirarchi

ROBERTA'S / BLANCA, BUSHWICK
40.70507° N, 73.93359° W

In modern-day Brooklyn, all roads lead to Roberta's, the restaurant that crystallized Bushwick's status as the heart of creative Brooklyn. Everybody has worked there, eaten there, or wished they'd done one of the two. Its influence cannot be understated, and is due in large part to its iconoclastic chef Carlo Mirarchi, who couldn't have anticipated that making some of the city's finest pizza and small plates in a stripped-bare, graffitied warehouse would help shape the landscape of the borough, and the way people eat around the world.

But he and his business partners opened Roberta's way back in 2008. These days, he helms a two-Michelin-starred tasting counter, Blanca, in Roberta's backyard, and reckons with what it means now that Roberta's has its own line of supermarket frozen pizzas and high-profile financial investors, all while making sure the anti-establishment restaurant doesn't lose what made it unique in the first place.

How did you first get interested in cooking?

I came from a very food-oriented family. My mom's from Panama and my dad's from Italy, so I was exposed to food at a really young age. I got my first restaurant job when I was 16 as a busboy and dishwasher.

Where was that?

At a pizza place on Long Island—a red sauce joint. I loved everything about it. I guess I just got hooked when I was pretty young. I wanted to keep on working at restaurants but my parents were not very happy with that. They were both immigrants and didn't want me to work in restaurants. This was in the early 1990s and I was just graduating high school.

What happened once you graduated high school?

I got a scholarship to go to New York University, so I went to school and I did whatever random restaurant work I could, including catering work. When I graduated, I worked with *Vice* for a little bit, then got a job at one of the first Scandinavian restaurants in the city. That was my first real restaurant job; it just felt really natural to me. I really enjoyed it. It felt like the only thing I was ever really good at.

How did Roberta's get started in Bushwick?

When I lived in the area in the early 2000s, a friend of mine, Brandon Hoy, who I had known just through bars, restaurants, and several mutual friends, told me he had found a space in beautiful Bushwick, Brooklyn with Chris [Parachini] and they were looking for another partner, someone who would handle the food part. I came to check it out, we started talking, and it just worked out.

What was Bushwick like in 2007 when you were first opening Roberta's?

Honestly, the vibe didn't feel that different from what it is now. There were just fewer people. At night, you wouldn't see people walking around or anything like that. There wasn't anywhere to go.

When we opened it was just so empty. We didn't have money. We couldn't fix things that were broken. It was difficult to get reps to come out here and sell to us. It was hard to even set up accounts with people at the farmers' market because they didn't know where we were, or hadn't heard of us before and didn't believe us. It just sounded crazy to a lot of people.

Were there any other restaurants in the area?

There were a couple places on Wyckoff. Northeast Kingdom [a restaurant] was around before we were too, but really, there was nothing here.

If you were to open a new restaurant in Bushwick now, do you think you'd have the same difficulty?

I think it's hard to open a restaurant anywhere. I don't think it matters where you are. I'm sure some of those logistical challenges are a bit easier now, but there would be different types of difficulties.

What, if any, impact do you think Roberta's had on the neighborhood?

I don't know. I feel like the neighborhood changes with the people who move here, since it's a comfortable, reasonable place for people to live. There have been communities here for a long time—my dad used to live on Halsey Street in the 1960s and 1970s. But the kind of people here have shifted over time. I think it ebbs and flows, just like any other neighborhood.

When you opened Roberta's, the menu was predominantly Italian-style cooking. Was that impacted at all by any of the Italian restaurants you worked at in the past?

Not really. It was more because we had such limited space in the kitchen. We didn't have any gas, and we had very little electricity available. We were just trying to figure out what we could make work in a difficult kitchen. I had to cook a lot of stuff in the wood-burning oven, because we didn't have any ovens, and I had to use what we had.

When Roberta's first opened, what was the menu like?

It was a lot smaller. We had maybe six to eight different pizzas, and then 10 to 12 kitchen items that rotated. Because it changed so frequently, we did a handwritten menu every day.

How did you first get people to come to the restaurant?

The first two years, it was really tough to get people to come in. We didn't have a liquor license, and it got cold in the winter. It was mostly neighborhood people who came in at first.

How do you think people outside of the neighborhood started hearing about you?

I think word of mouth mostly, and then a really nice write-up brought more people into the fold.

It's amazing that, in just shy of a decade, a pizza restaurant grew to include Blanca, a two Michelin-starred restaurant. It seems that there are a lot of restaurants now that have a high-end restaurant and lower-end, casual restaurant running simultaneously.

New York City is a very expensive place to operate a restaurant, and it's getting more and more difficult to have a middle-of-the-road restaurant, or a restaurant that aims really high. You need to have some kind of balance of something that's fast casual, with good margins, in order for you to do more high-level stuff that probably has little to no margin.

Did you always intend to open Blanca?

No, not really. It just happened organically.

What about the chef's table at Roberta's?

We actually started that because of David Kinch [chef of Manresa in California]. We met at an event that we were doing, and whenever he was in New York, he would come by. I would just cook up a menu for him, and he would always say, "Hey, you should do this for more people." He started sending some of his regular guests who lived in New York or spent time in New York to come in, and it just started growing from there.

How would you describe your food at Blanca by comparison?

To me, they're similar, because it's all my food. But I think any differences are a matter of the menu format: it's a difference in rhythms and flavors, what the meal revolves around. At Roberta's, I tend to go for bigger flavors and aim for more acidity. Blanca is probably a little subtler, and I think more about not only what you're eating right now but also what you ate before and what you'll eat after.

Has the size of the tasting menu at Blanca evolved over the years, or has it always been the same?

In the beginning we were super ambitious and wanted to do 30 courses and all this stuff with ingredients I had always wanted to work with. We weren't necessarily being considerate of using our time in the right way. Like anything, it takes a while to find your rhythm and find the place where you're comfortable working. I think it definitely has become more focused in the last two or three years. At one point, we had 26 courses, and now we're probably at 16 or 18, depending. It's still a lot.

Would people describe Roberta's as an Italian restaurant?

I don't know. I've always wondered that. I guess, for me, as far as the food goes, we use a Southern Italian approach to ingredients and technique. So, while you may not recognize a dish or the exact ingredients or anything like that, I guess I like to say that it's maybe how an Italian person would cook in New York, which I am and which I do.

What do mean by a Southern Italian approach?

It's more minimalist, and we don't use a lot of dairy. We also pick all of our own herbs, from coriander to purple basil, Thai basil, sunflower, and all different kinds of mints.

Would you say the pizza at Roberta's is more New York-style or Neapolitan-style?

It's definitely not a Neapolitan style, we're not that strict about it, especially with some of the toppings we do and stuff. I think it's more how a New York person would do a Neapolitan-influenced pie.

What's the difference between the different pizza styles?

I'm a very big fan of a New York-style slice of pizza. It's almost like comparing a New York-style hot dog to a German bratwurst or something. Or a Tex-Mex taco to what we would have in Mexico City. They're just completely and totally different.

The biggest difference is that you can't get a slice of Neapolitan-style pizza. It comes from a place of tradition where there's a very specific value system around it. Essentially, what I recognize, besides the obvious differences, the wood fire and all that stuff, is just the dough itself. The New York-style slice is very crisp—really, really crisp—and well-proportioned between sauce, cheese, and the actual process. A Neapolitan pie, in my mind, comes from wood fire. A lot of times, it's going to be naturally fermented, so a lot more of the flavor comes from the dough. You can have mozzarella on a Neapolitan pie, which is totally different. It's a little bit more of an actual eating experience as opposed to something you would have late at night, or after a bar or while you're walking home. It's also not something I think that people necessarily would want to eat every day, because it is, to me,

something kind of special. It's definitely more of an experience.

Of the menus at Roberta's and Blanca, do you have a favorite dish?

It changes seasonally. We have a watermelon and Crenshaw melon dish at Blanca that I really like that's with a sunflower nut curd. The other one I like is nectarine juice with almonds, and then at Roberta's a watermelon and avocado salad with black lime. I like those a lot in the summer.

What inspires the menu?

We're a team, so we operate as a team. It's the same with Roberta's. It's a lot of throwing ideas around, working with ingredients, and just tasting over and over and over again.

Is that easier to do in the summer?

I think summer is my favorite season to cook—probably between May or June until late September. You just have a little bit more ingredients to work with. I like the fall a lot, too. I like cooking meat, but I just feel like I have a little more fun and interesting things to play around with that time of year.

If you could eat anywhere right now, where would you go?

Probably Pujol [in Mexico City]. I think I was last there a year or two ago.

Where do you usually go out to eat?

It's probably going to be Thai or Japanese. I actually really, really love Night + Market in Los Angeles. It's one of my favorite restaurants, I really like Jon & Vinny's out in Los Angeles too. Usually, when I go out to eat, I don't want anything similar to what we make here. I go to Cosme a lot, as well as Ten Bells and Blue Smoke. Outside of that, I mostly eat at work. There are so many restaurants I would love to go to, but I just don't have enough time.

If you could cook for anybody, who would it be and why?

I'm a really, really big Nick Cave fan. He's a musician from Australia, so I'd love to cook for him. I would really like to make pasta, maybe for Valentino Rossi, who's a motorcycle racer that I really like. I have a feeling he really enjoys pasta. For the Mugello race, his helmet was emblazoned with rigatoni. It was pretty awesome.

On the Side
By Giuseppe Lacorazza

I arrived to Nicolás Losada's apartment in Bed-Stuy. An old childhood friend kind enough to let me stay with him, he lived at the time with his bandmate, Juli, and a tattooed vegan couple in their mid-thirties who fostered two cats. I came to New York to train in the kitchen of the famous (and now closed) restaurant wd-50, and work at the soon-to-be-opened restaurant Contra, both in the Lower East Side of Manhattan.

Nico, a trained jazz musician who led the band Salt Cathedral, had been living in Brooklyn for a year. At the time, he worked part-time at Pizza Moto, a pizzeria pop-up with a wood-fired oven built on top of a trailer. He's not a skillful cook, and he was never interested in food, restaurants, or their philosophy until he had to find a job to support his musical career.

But he is now.

As I worked in different restaurants, made friends, and tried again and again to find cheap rents I could afford with my kitchen salary, I learned to love Brooklyn. (I also couldn't afford a Manhattan apartment.) In Brooklyn, I found myself surrounded by countless artistic young people — writers, musicians, and filmmakers. They've been my co-workers, housemates, neighbors, and friends. And I've realized that Nico's newborn interest in the restaurant world wasn't uncommon among artists. In fact, these young artists, who collect their service industry paychecks to support their art, are the servers and cooks who sustain the New York restaurant industry. And they mostly live in Brooklyn.

I read in the New York Times that, while working as a bartender at The Odeon, Andrew Tarlow, one of Brooklyn's most influential chef-restaurateurs, "admired the way the [Odeon's] owner, Lynn Wagenknecht, created a neighborhood gathering place for artists. It inspired his vision for the once-desolate streets of Williamsburg." Tarlow grew to own an empire that includes restaurants, an indie apparel store, a literary magazine, and a hotel that hosts a Food Book Fair. He realized his businesses were not only places where the young artists living around the neighborhood gathered, but also a space where they could work. He embraced the new focus of food as an intellectual, political, and artistic tool— and he ran with it, leading many others to follow suit on their own terms.

At Roberta's, for example, the atmosphere is closer to a DIY show at Silent Barn (an underground performance art space in Brooklyn) than it is to a meal at any other serious restaurant—likely because staffers and customers are closer to the Brooklyn art scene than the restaurant industry. It's the only restaurant I know that has a tiki bar, a hidden two-Michelin-starred chef's counter, and a radio station in a shipping container with a dining room view. Despite the artsy, fun-loving atmosphere, Roberta's takes its food very, very seriously. That duality has defined Roberta's, and has given it a distinctive personality that couldn't have come out of the traditional, more formal model of running a kitchen. That palpable mixture of the art and food worlds colliding makes it a distinctly Brooklyn restaurant (or, a "Hipster Italian dining plus takeout," according to Google Maps).

Young and broke New York artists have long had to find jobs to support their dreams. Restaurants, which often suffer from a shortage of reliable, talented staff, have always been there to welcome them. (Jay Z, whose picture as a working teenager hangs in the window of a Crown Fried Chicken in Myrtle Avenue, was one of them.). This hasn't changed. What's different now is that food is *cooler* than it's ever been. For the first time, it seems that some artists are no longer thinking of their part-time food industry jobs as a side hustle for financial support. Now that the borough of the last decade has a more overt creative spirit, young artists happily embrace the service industry and, as a result, help shape its future.

Bushwick-based musician Bryan Wade Keller, Jr. started serving tables at Roberta's in 2011. Bryan's various jobs include touring with his band Softspot, producing music, collaborating with his partner, performance artist Sarah Kinlaw, and now unexpectedly working

as a sommelier. "I realized that since I was going to be spending a lot of time in restaurants, I wanted to at least learn something from them," he told me while polishing wine glasses at Wildair, the wine bar on the Lower East Side of Manhattan where we both work now.

At Roberta's, where he previously worked, Amanda Smeltz (a poet turned sommelier) introduced him to natural wines, and he has been obsessed with learning about them ever since. "I see it now as an alternative career path," he says, adding that while music is still his main focus, wine and hospitality have become a passion for him, instead of just a secondary career that helps him maintain creative freedom with his music.

For illustrator and restaurant veteran Erika Da Silva, it was the melting pot of cultures and backgrounds in the restaurants that fascinated her. "Food is a connector," she told me. She first started working in restaurants after journalism school as a way to meet people and make her monthly rent. But the meeting people part kept her in the business.

While she was working at a hotel restaurant, one of the dishwashers suddenly passed away. "He was from Puebla; it turned out that most of the workers there were as well," she says, noting that he was also dating a front-of-house worker. "It began a collective mourning process, with rituals that included the workers' wives bringing traditional foods daily for everyone. I had never seen anything like that before. That was it for me. I realized I could meet more people from different backgrounds working in restaurants than I would in any other job."

Erika went from server to restaurant manager to founder of Crown 9 Studios, where she hand-paints lively scenes and floral portraits with a strong use of watercolors. Many of her subjects and clients are, inevitably, food-related.

Even diners have come to expect food to be presented with a touch of artistic expression, rather than just a commodity. This is not an exclusively local phenomenon; it's just, as many things are, intensified in New York City.

The realization that there's an audience that looks for a different approach to their dining experiences in turn inspires the creative people working in those restaurants. And, in Brooklyn, it has created a perfect platform for eclectic food businesses to sprout. It's no longer necessary to lean on the established rubrics for uber-expensive fine dining or neighborhood hole-in-the-wall restaurants of old New York.

With rent skyrocketing in Manhattan, and a workforce of young dreamers looking for financial aid, Brooklyn has become the perfect place to land these new-age food projects and established artists have taken notice.

Last year James Murphy, the founder of Brooklyn-born cult-favorite band LCD Soundsystem, opened The Four Horsemen, a natural wine bar in Williamsburg with a minimalist design and a dynamic small-plates menu. In Bushwick, artists Jen Monroe and Caroline Polachek host monochromatic dinner parties that include performance art pieces by other local artists. And Dave Arnold's longtime project, The Museum of Food and Drink, opened its first physical space just south of McCarren Park with an exhibit about the history of the flavor industry.

"People want the same thing out of food that they want out of art," says Lexie Smith, a baker, illustrator, and sculptor, whose food career has given her a better platform to present her art. "I get attention for cooking and I get paid to do it. Then I tell people that I also do art, and that they should care about it too. And they do."

In a time when documenting and sharing what we eat is an integral part of social interaction, and in a place where people are willing to eat out as often as monetarily possible, food in New York becomes a vehicle for personal and social identity. It is an unwritten language that conveys who we are and what we like. It is, ultimately, an information source, a tool used by politicians, businessmen, and activists.

Now artists are starting to consciously use it too: for Lexie, as a utilitarian vehicle for self-expression when she sculpted with bread dough; for Erika, as an anthropological experience; for Jen and Caroline, as a new perspective for experimental performance; and, for many others, as an economic safety net.

Food, as a medium of cultural and historical documentation, can be used to explore Brooklyn's current artistic reality. And art can, in turn, continue to inject restaurants with necessary creativity. It doesn't mean food is art. In fact, all of the people with whom I spoke made it clear I should separate the two. But right now, these distinct communities overlap in Brooklyn, the epicenter of the city's creative output, where young artists reinvent the borough's restaurant scene while they reinvent themselves.

Photography by Heidi's Bridge

Andrew Tarlow

MARLOW & SONS, ACHILLES HEEL, DINER, ROMAN'S, WYTHE HOTEL, SHE WOLF BAKERY

Since Andrew Tarlow opened his first restaurant Diner in Williamsburg in 1998, he has established himself as the man who best understands what a Brooklyn neighborhood restaurant should look, taste, and feel like. Again and again, he's opened restaurants (he now has six, including Marlow & Sons and Achilles Heel, plus the Wythe Hotel, a butcher shop, and She Wolf Bakery), that, on opening day, seem as organic to the community as its street signs and bodegas. In 18 years, the borough has become almost unrecognizable—and yet, Tarlow and his restaurants adapt, proliferate, and thrive, without pandering to fads. We spoke with Tarlow, who just published a cookbook, *Dinner at the Long Table*, about how he's built a Brooklyn empire with approachable food, prepared expertly, and in good company.

How did you get into the restaurant business?

I didn't always know this was what I wanted. I was fascinated by food and restaurants for a long time. I went to, and threw, lots of dinner parties. I loved taking care of people around a table. Those things were all there for me. But it wasn't until an old diner on my corner became available, and the barrier to entry for owning a restaurant was really low, that it happened. Nobody was watching or paying attention to Brooklyn at the time, so it allowed me to think about community instead of food costs. I could take care of my neighbors instead of worrying about labor overhead. I'm really lucky that I was able to approach it that way from the beginning.

What was it like opening that first restaurant?

My first restaurant, Diner, is going to be 18 years old. It started as a rundown restaurant on a rundown corner of Williamsburg. We took it over, unearthed what was here, remodeled it, and brought the space back to life. What we learned was that we could look back at the past, see what's good, and figure out what should be saved and what should go.

When you first opened Diner, what did you have in mind for the restaurant?

We weren't even that ambitious at that time. We just wanted to get food to a table and make sure a fork and knife would be placed next to the food.

You mentioned that you've been able to determine which ideas should stay and which should go. What kinds of ideas have you scrapped?

At one point, I thought about an Airstream, because I was worried that the citywide smoking ban would kill my business and no one would ever go out again. I thought I could just run food across the street. I'll also say that we had lots of good ideas that we're upset we don't do anymore.

What was the New York dining scene like when you opened Diner in 1998?

The dining world was really focused on Manhattan, and almost entirely focused on fine dining chefs. We needed Danny [Meyer] to move things more lo-fi. In that context, we had the opportunity to respond to this on the fly, and just define it as we went.

What was Williamsburg like?

At the time, there were tons of people living around here in illegal lofts. It has informed so much of what we do. Everyone back then was just happy to have a place to go. We created a community for a bunch of people who didn't know each other. It happened for me too. I was living down the street, and I didn't know anybody who lived here. We immediately found that we became a gathering spot that forged friendships. To this day, it has allowed our restaurants to have a different mission statement.

It would be one thing if you had just one successful, influential restaurant. But you have six—plus a bakery, a butcher, and a hotel. How do you maintain quality and consistency when you open a new place?

That's a hard one. If I could figure out the exact way to do that, I'd probably be a lot more successful. One thing I know: I don't build restaurants that are concept-based. People are always like, "What's the new thing? What's the concept?" I don't approach my job or my next restaurant with that mindset. Because none of the restaurants are concept-driven, we don't have to wear certain shirts or act a certain way. I feel like some restaurant owners dive into French brasseries as if they're

Roman's

Diner

Diner

Keith McNally and then into Asian fusion, and they think dressing people up makes it different and on-theme or something.

I have no urge to do that. If I were to open a Japanese-inspired restaurant, I wouldn't dress anyone up in an outfit, or force them to speak Japanese, or make the interior feel like it's from Japan. I work more organically. Ideas that come to fruition are usually based on people who are employed here. The new places may allow them to take the next step in their career. I see myself as a conduit or producer of those things, rather than the person who is a lone genius behind the scenes at a board table.

How do you know when it's the right time to open a new place?

I open pretty slowly. You really have to have good real estate to begin with for a new place to work. We're very disciplined in getting the right real estate. That's the piece of the puzzle that comes before anything else. If you do that first, I think you have a much better chance of getting it right. The next thing is to have really good people. You not only have to hire them, but you have to assemble a good crew and give them promotions and enable them to grow and take the next step.

How much do consumer tastes drive those new restaurants?

We're not really motivated by trends. There's always the expectation that I'll continue to open things. But I haven't opened anything new in two-and-a-half years. I own a lot, but I've been so blessed and lucky that it's been a slow tour. People sometimes ask me, "So, what are you doing?" And I just tell them I'm running these businesses, and there's a lot of work that goes into that.

What kind of work happens on a day-to-day basis?

Hiring great people and keeping them inspired is harder than it sounds. You have to constantly self-evaluate and reflect. You have to take care of people still—customers and staff—and you have to find joy in the day to day. There's so much to it.

When I'm not opening new things, I'm thoughtful about continuing to raise my children here. When I'm opening something new, I'm considering how my team will feel about it. I can't just walk away. Having a restaurant is kind of like having a kid: You have to be prepared to raise that kid, and not just have some nanny raise it for you. You can do that and it'll turn out just fine. But, do you love this thing enough that you'll want to be home at 4 p.m.?

You've been a Brooklyn resident for a long time. How has it felt as a resident and a business owner over the last several decades?

I've been living in Brooklyn for about 25 years. I would say that if you're not someone who is adept at dealing with or willing to live with change, living here is difficult. I've obviously taken the upside on the success this borough has had, and in that capacity, I think it's great. I don't love living in a construction zone, and I don't love every building that's ever been built, but I think what's happening in Williamsburg provides context to what's happening in this borough and all over the city right now.

Do you still feel like you're part of your neighborhood's community?

I don't have strong feelings about the borough and the landscape, but I have strong feelings for things that I can have an effect on. As an example, I'm for grass-fed beef. The commodity beef market is bad for us and our planet, so I'll make sure we only purchase animals directly from farms I trust, and that they get paid within two weeks.

Do you eat at your restaurants?

I'm going to go to Diner tonight actually. One way you can really control quality is by eating at your own places. It's a great way to understand what's going on. I have trouble finding time to go out to eat and check out new restaurants, or even see my friends. Having children—literal and figurative—makes it hard.

Diner

Achilles Heel

Reynard

An Afternoon at Gloria's
By Angela Almeida & John Surico

At Gloria's Caribbean Cuisine, there is one menu to rule them all.

It is a sprawling, illuminated board on the wall, as if taken from some lost Caribbean diner from the 1950s, featuring a faded illustration of a roti roll drawn under the tagline, "Love at first bite." From the looks of it, the menu items—including roti, curried goat, and callaloo—have persevered; their penciled-in prices, which still rarely surpass $10, maybe not so much. And before regulars even make it to the counter, some pause to reassess their hunger: Is it time to switch things up, or stay the course?

But then, there are the veterans, unyielding in their lifelong orders. Some have been coming to Gloria's since it first opened over four decades ago at its original outpost further down Nostrand Avenue. There are now three locations, but this one, on the corner of Nostrand and Sterling Street, in Crown Heights, has become the unspoken flagship. Though it's nowhere near the beaches of Trinidad, Gloria's is a Brooklyn institution of such mouth-watering West Indian cuisine that, when locals debate authenticity, the place seems closer to those far-off beaches than ever.

Gloria's feels more like a corner shack than a restaurant. In the summertime, the small, square store—with only enough room for a few tables and a counter—makes its presence known with perpetually open floor-to-ceiling windows beckoning customers on the streets with the pungent smells of tamarind and cumin. In the afternoons and evenings, it gets packed, reggae playing from a sound system in the corner, providing apropos island vibes—as if the plantains weren't enough.

The menu offers Caribbean classics like curried chicken or stewed oxtail, which, at Gloria's, naturally falls off the bone. That oxtail is basked in thyme, peppers, scallions, celery, and shado beni for seasoning, then seared, braised, and served, like everything else, over a bed of rice and peas, and in a tin foil container.

But Gloria's is smack dab in the middle of a neighborhood that is changing, perhaps faster than any other in Brooklyn. Once a predominantly Caribbean community, with Nostrand Avenue as its central vein, Crown Heights today is grappling with its identity. It is a classic case of gentrification, except thrown into hyper-drive. New, mostly white residents are moving in, and older Caribbean mainstays are moving out. Except for Gloria's.

"Customers are the ones that are helping us stay open," Bryan Cumberbatch, the third-generation owner of Gloria's, told us. "We treat them like they're our best friends."

Cumberbatch grew up in the kitchen of Gloria's, which is named after his grandmother, who opened up the first shop in 1973. "Back then," he said, "she had the only West Indian restaurant that was open." The loving matriarch had come from Trinidad, Bryan added. She brought with her four children and a host of recipes that have lived on long past her death in 2005.

Among those are the callaloo, a seasoned blend of spinach, okra, coconut milk, and pumpkin, and the dhal, made up of chickpeas. "You boil it down. You season it—we say bungie it in Trinidad," Cumberbatch said. "That means you burn the garlic in [the dhal] to give it that flavor. Sometimes we wake up in the morning and just drink a cup of that."

And, of course, there's the roti. For Ross Otto, 33, the veggie rendition of this fluffy Caribbean flat bread is worth every penny, which is why, even after moving out of the neighborhood two years ago, he finds himself back in Crown Heights often. It's also why, before he relocates to Montreal, the white, non-native Brooklynite is currently getting his fix. "Before I go," he admitted, "I had to binge."

When Ross lived here, he frequented Gloria's sometimes twice a week, swapping out cereal for the traditional Trinidadian bake and saltfish breakfast. "When I bring out-of-towners here, they just think West Indies food is jerk chicken," he explained. "And then they

come to Gloria's, and it blows their mind."

It's the kind of place that leaves an impression, which is why it didn't go unnoticed for too long. In 2012, Anthony Bourdain stopped here on his show, "No Reservations," a televised moment that lent credence to the notion that Gloria's was something special. Not only did Bourdain's visit widen its customer base, particularly to those who were just moving into the neighborhood, it also cemented the restaurant's reputation beyond the block.

Though for patrons like Joseph Archbold, 47, who has been coming here for the past thirty years, that wasn't really necessary.

"When I feel like roti, this is my stop," Archbold said, a Crown Heights native who now lives in the nearby neighborhood of East New York. "I just come to get the food, then turn around and get back on the 3 train home."

Archbold is a potato and channa roti enthusiast, but lately, his options have been limited. Although Gloria's has lasted, the local Caribbean holes-in-the-wall that he grew up with have closed down, he said, as the area experiences an influx of pricier eateries. And across the city, too, newer, more expensive Caribbean joints—like Miss Lily's in Manhattan, and even Gladys, down the block from Gloria's—have become popular. So it's not as if the cuisine is necessarily vanishing, but rather, being muted to appeal to a more mimosa-maddened crowd, which, of course, raises complex questions of what is culturally authentic.

Yet within this changing landscape, Gloria's has not only survived but, also, thrived. Four years ago, Cumberbatch started online food deliveries to adapt to the at-your-doorstep Seamless culture, and recently, he has settled on opening a new Harlem location, bringing his family's famous fare out of Brooklyn for the first time. "In the future, I plan to take it to another level," he said. "Probably open one in every state."

That might sound like a huge undertaking, especially when considering that Gloria's currently has just three locations, but much of Cumberbatch's confidence comes from what he sees as its global appeal. Like one of his regulars, a German customer he's never met, who orders a $1,000 worth of food every two weeks. "We ship it. We pack it," he said. "We get the food sealer, and [we] seal it up nice."

"We don't cater to one kind of person," Cumberbatch continued. "[Gloria's is] an international thing. It's something for everybody to enjoy."

Maybe that's what has kept it intact. Whether for newcomers, regulars, or the British tourists we met when we last ate there, Gloria's feels like a savory safe haven. You come for the food and you stay for the food. Just like the roti, this is where a community folds into itself: where the forces of change are kept at bay, too busy staring up at the menu board, while the food, its most sacred identity, stays the same.

When asked what he thinks Gloria's secret for survival is, Cumberbatch admitted, "To tell you the truth, sometimes I wonder how we do it."

The Soda Fountain
By Blair Pfander

"People ask me all the time, 'Is there egg in this?'"

Carmine Morales has been serving egg creams—the bygone Brooklyn soda fountain staple and effervescent cousin of the milkshake—to customers at Classic Coffee Shop since 1976, when he opened his two-table luncheonette on New York's Lower East Side.

After 40 years, Morales, who speaks in an old-school *Noo Yawk* accent, decided to settle the issue once and for all. He added a disclaimer to the back of his menu that reads, "EGG CREAM: DOES NOT CONTAIN EGGS."

Yet customers still ask. An egg cream consists of three simple ingredients: Soda water. Chocolate syrup. Cold milk. Zero eggs.

In its 1950s heyday, New Yorkers could find egg creams at any soda fountain, corner, or diner in the five boroughs—the latter of which were largely owned by Greek or Jewish American families. The drink's American immigrant heritage is reflected in the lore surrounding its peculiar misnomer, which has been passed down through generations of soda jerks, busboys, and diner owners.

One popular theory claims that "egg cream" is an American bastardization of *echt keem*, or "pure sweetness" in Yiddish. Another is that 19th century actor Boris Thomashefsky requested a "chocolat et creme," a sweet treat he'd enjoyed in Paris at his local soda fountain, but the request got lost in translation.

Other theories point to hygienic advances. "From my experience in the restaurant business I believe it started with eggs in it and probably real cream, but I'm sure we wised up about raw eggs and it transformed over time," says Billy Tourloukis, manager at Tom's Diner in Prospect Heights (where, he's quick to point out, egg creams have been on the menu for 80 years).

Whatever its true origins, the egg cream recipe is humble. It starts with a hearty squirt of chocolate syrup—purists know that only Fox's U-Bet will do. (Made in Brooklyn since the early 20th century, Fox's is less sweet yet seemingly silkier than Hershey's.) The drizzle of syrup is followed by a splash of ice-cold whole milk. Then it's finished with a shock of seltzer, ideally blasted from a soda gun, and followed by a powerful stir to create a frothy head. It is sweet, but not overpowering. It is fizzy, but easy to sip.

But in 2016, the once-ubiquitous egg cream has become difficult to find, even in the borough that birthed it.

"I get customers coming in here who used to live in New York and remember the egg cream but haven't had one for years. You can't find them so much anymore," laments Carmine.

A possible explanation for the egg cream's dwindling popularity is that as Coca-Cola and Pepsi grew in the 1970s—making sweet, bubbly beverages available at grocery stores—they demolished demand for soda shops. As the soda shops disappeared, so did egg creams.

However, in some hip, new establishments dedicated to embodying a certain brand of Brooklyn nostalgia, the egg cream is making a comeback. Carroll Garden's Brooklyn Farmacy—a turn-of-the-last-century time warp on Henry Street, complete with tin ceilings and white-capped waitresses—charges $3 for a classic U-Bet version and $4 for a version that caters to its stylish clientele: a handcrafted, specialty egg cream with ingredients like coffee, maple syrup, and non-dairy milk.

Some of the egg cream's rekindled popularity might be attributed to the fact that Brooklyn itself is in vogue. It's a sweet souvenir from a simpler, tougher borough, where kids bought them at bodegas along with Spalding balls and cigarettes. When I ask Tourloukis, who orders egg creams on the menu at Tom's, he explains, "There's a lot of nostalgia involved. The neighborhood people order them but so do the tourists."

Brooklynites tend to remember their first egg cream as vividly as they remember Ebbets Field. "Believe it or not, I had my

first egg cream on Manhattan Avenue at Woolworth's," says Donna Siafakas, the affable co-owner of Brooklyn institution, Peter Pan Bakery, where customers line up down the block for warm, hand-cut donuts served by smiling waitresses in mint-green smocks.

Like Carmine, Siafakas skips her R's. "We called it the five and dime," she explains. "They had a luncheonette counter"—*countah*—"where you could sit down for a break while you shopped. The egg creams cost about ten cents, and I remember"—*remembah*—"them being served in a paper cone-shaped cup with an insert. They would throw away the insert for the next customer. It was really very sanitary."

Speaking with diner owners like Siafakas, it seems the egg cream belongs less to the early 20th century fantasy of Brooklyn, conjured by places like Brooklyn Farmacy, than to this memory of a working-class Brooklyn childhood. "A Brooklyn kid never quits dreaming of stickball triples, egg creams, and the funnies," Jonathan Lethem wrote in *The Fortress of Solitude*. King of New York cool, the Velvet Underground's Lou Reed, rhapsodized about sipping the drink as a boy in his song, "Egg Cream":

When I was a young man, no bigger than this /
A chocolate egg cream was not to be missed /
Some U Bet's Chocolate Syrup, seltzer water mixed with milk /
Stir it up into a head fro—tasted just like silk.

To many Brooklyn stalwarts, the egg cream never went away—at least not to the loyal customers who depend on it. Classic Coffee Shop "still gets the egg cream regulars," says Morales. And at Peter Pan Donuts, "it's really always been the same," says Siafakas. "We've always had a steady egg cream customer." Certain regulars, she adds, have been ordering it "for decades."

Fortunately for egg cream enthusiasts, the drink is easy enough to make at home. First, get your hands on some U-Bet (Amazon stocks it on Prime delivery). Place an eight-ounce glass in the freezer until the glass is frosted over. Spoon an inch of chocolate syrup into the bottom, and cover that with another inch of milk. Top with seltzer. Consider sipping on your stoop for maximum effect.

L'Chayim:
The Life of Delis
By Jonathan Shipley

"I have pastrami in my blood," says Jake Dell, a man who thought he would be a doctor. Instead, Dell became the owner of what is arguably the most famous Jewish deli in the world, Manhattan's Katz's Delicatessen. He's the fifth generation owner, and his lineage stretches back to the deli's founding in 1888. "The deli called," he says. "It's a tradition that I take seriously."

Meanwhile, in Brooklyn, Aaron Israel is in the kitchen with his wife, Sawako Okochi, at their restaurant Shalom Japan shaking up that tradition. Their place, which opened in the summer of 2013, is a fusion of Japanese and Jewish food. Whereas Katz's serves the same pastrami sandwich it did in 1888, Israel and Okochi serve sake kasu challah, matzo ball ramen, and a lox bowl with rice and Japanese pickles.

"The main tradition of Jewish food is the idea of adaptation and change," Israel says. "There's nothing inherently Jewish about Gefilte fish. It's a Hungarian dish Jewish people adapted. There is nothing even particularly Jewish about a matzo ball. It's an adaptation of German bread dumplings."

If you were living in New York City in the 1930s, you couldn't go a city block without passing by a Jewish deli—the smell of fork tender meats, pickles, freshly baked breads, and hot soups. There were approximately 1,500 delis in the city in the 1930s. Now, according to Ted Merwin, author of the definitive history of the Jewish deli, *Pastrami on Rye,* there are approximately 15 proper Jewish delis left in New York City. And the few that remain fall into one of two camps: the famous holdouts that welcome tourists and the spunky up-and-comers eager to put new spins on old classics.

The deli boom in New York coincided with its growing population—more than one million newcomers arrived on Ellis Island in 1907, the city's peak year for immigration. Many of these immigrants were of European and Jewish descent. Feeling like outsiders, they congregated in certain neighborhoods throughout the city: the Lower East Side, Murray Hill, Borough Park, Crown Heights, and Williamsburg. They were looking for "third places"— those environments between work and home—where they could commiserate and chat with like-minded individuals about how the New York Yankees could win the pennant. Harpo Marx once described delis as home to a mix of "card players, horseplayers, bookies, song-pluggers, agents, actors out of work and actors playing the Palace, Al Jolson with his mob of fans, and Arthur Rothstein with his mob of runners and flunkies." Just as the Irish imported to New York City the pub and the Italians the social clubs of Little Italy, the Jews brought with them delis, replete with sandwiches piled high, hot soup, and steady conversation.

Jay Parker, proprietor of Ben's Best in Queens takes pride in offering his services to the community and by being an integral part of it. "The kosher deli has a special place in the Jewish community, a place to keep the culture of the religion alive. Holidays, weddings, and bar and bat mitzvahs are all significant to our community. We must be there for them."

Navigating the evolving tastes and attitudes of today's clientele, while offering the comforting food of established tradition is a difficult task, but one delis are interested in taking on. "So if you take noodle pudding, batter dip it and drizzle demi-glace over it, the question then is, is it still noodle pudding?" asks Parker from Ben's Best.

But a rising tide lifts all ships. "Anything that advances the industry is good for the industry." Most owners, Dell and Parker included, seem to agree that the new delis, with their newer noodle puddings and spins of matzo ball soups, can offer eaters what traditional delis cannot. And, more importantly, it brings a younger audience into delis and establishes a connection to food—and a tradition—they may not have known otherwise.

But those newer places are trying to find their niche among the traditional delis such as Sarge's, Ben's Best, and Katz's. "What makes good Jewish food good is what makes any food good: caring about

it on all levels," Israel states. "Good ingredients, respect of the product, and putting the love into it make a great final product. Sprinkling in a little nostalgia doesn't hurt either."

Ultimately, the deli scene in New York City is hurting. Delis, like Katz's and those now gone—Cheesecake Sam's, Reuben's, Max's Stage Delicatessen, Brooklyn on Rye, Ester Deli— were places where shoe shiners could buff up against New York's elite in a place where they were all equals. That sort of cross-section is what still interests deli owners to this day, but it's becoming harder and harder to come by.

Community is hard to build and maintain when delis close or move out of the city, as a result of high rents, struggling economies, and shifting priorities of the Jewish community. The immigrants of the 1920s and 1930s needed work, so they took jobs requiring physical labor, which demanded long hours with slim profit margins. "My grandparents," Parker says, "knew that they were sacrificing their lives for the next generation, insisting on educating the children and demanding they do better." In that way, the demise of the industry is a happy conclusion.

"For 128 years we've been serving the same sandwich, the same knish, the same hot dog," Dell says. Like all New York deli owners, he's proud of the work he does and is eager to put together another sandwich and offer it to an actor, a bookie, a tourist, a tramp as they sit, together, at the deli—a place not quite like home but, thankfully, not quite like any other place either.

At Jay & Lloyd's Kosher Deli in Sheepshead Bay, hungry Brooklynites still sit down to chopped liver salad and tongue polonaise—a far cry from the avocado toasts young people huddle around in Manhattan. But in the proud outer reaches of the borough, the two self-proclaimed mensches who own it—just like many of the remaining deli owners throughout the city—aren't altering their approach to suit trendy palates.

"I know we're on the right track," Parker says at Ben's Best, "when a customer tells us our food is 'almost as good as Bubby's.'"

Field 5
By Elena Sheppard

I grew up in Brooklyn where, truth be told, there are endless perks to an urban childhood. Mundane, daily tasks that seem like drudgery as an adult —subway rides, navigating busy sidewalks, street meat smells —feel like adventure to kids.

Until you meet people who grew up elsewhere, peculiarities to life as a city kid escape you. My school had 13 storeys and we never thought twice about it. Our school also did not have playing fields; we used city parks for that. Gym class was held in Cadman Plaza Park and home games were hosted on the ballparks in Red Hook.

Our softball team, the Saint Ann's Steamers, played on field 5, a field in Red Hook that is now cordoned off by the city for health reasons. We would arrive at field 5 in school buses and clear litter off the baselines. Our games were soundtracked by passing ice cream trucks, emergency vehicles, and the conversation wafting over from the surrounding housing projects—the arguments and laughter of strangers filling every potential silence with sound. We played on weekdays, when the fields were almost always full. Children and adults came from all over the borough to take advantage of a place to play.

On the weekends, that corner of Clinton and Bay Street was home to a conglomerate of stalls known as the Red Hook food vendors. Starting in the 1970s, those vendors came on weekends between April and October, making food for the soccer teams (and the spectators) that frequented the fields on Saturdays and Sundays. They created an oasis of Latin American street cuisine and operated much like the open air markets in the vendors' home countries of Mexico, Peru, Guatemala, and Honduras.

The stands were and are family run. One vendor told me on a recent visit that he started cooking in the '90s to help his mom with the weekend hustle. Another said she had been cooking on this corner for the past 15 years.

In the beginning, the vendors would drive from home with their grills and ingredients, setting up makeshift stalls under tarps in the park and serving pupusas, milkshakes, tacos, and tamales. It wasn't long before word spread, and the group got a reputation for serving some of the city's best Latin American street food. Because Red Hook in the 1980s and 1990s was still considered by many, or most, to be dangerous and remote, the city left the vendors alone to do their thing, to sell their snacks, and make their money.

No borough knows as well as Brooklyn how quickly neighborhoods can change. Red Hook, in less than 100 years, has gone from an active port to a slum area during the Depression to a blue collar hub during the '50s, a status immortalized in Arthur Miller's *A View From the Bridge*. By the 1990s, it was the epicenter of the crack epidemic, the neighborhood's housing projects synonymous with drugs and crime. Now in 2016 it's home to an Ikea, multi-million dollar homes, and a Fairway. Brooklyn knows well that nothing is forever.

What the present iteration of this transformation means for the Red Hook food vendors is that the city has stepped in. With neighborhood prices going up the city decided to pay attention and enforce rules previously ignored. Over the course of the past 10 years hygiene demands were upped and the Department of Health now requires food vendors to serve food from trucks rather than their traditional grill and table set-ups. The cost of even that change put a handful of the vendors immediately out of business. Think: roughly $50,000 to buy a truck, plus the gas required, plus the cost of a permit. For many, the sum was insurmountable.

Those who could, hung on and bought trucks from which to sell their Honduran baleadas and Mexican huaraches, slowly racking up mainstream food awards—including the coveted Vendy four times over—and proving to the city that they could play by the new rules that only came into effect as the neighborhood gentrified. Still, even with success, things have not gotten easier.

These days, the vendors still show up to the same corner on Saturdays and Sundays but business is way down. This has nothing to do with the food—still authentic, still delicious—and has everything to do with further restrictions implemented by the city. In 2015, the city shut down four of Red Hook's nine ball fields due to significant lead contamination. The lead is a remnant of the Columbia Smelting and Refining Works, which occupied much of the area in the '20s and '30s, refining scrap lead atop land that would one day be the playing fields.

The closures hit the vendors hard. Where there used to be 10 trucks on that corner, there are now five. Closed fields mean no games—and far fewer customers. One vendor, Marco, told me that people visiting the public Sol Goldman Pool (right next to the now locked field 5) keep them in business, but that profits are still down 30 to 40 percent. He also told me that the vendors collectively want to move closer to Ikea, where business would be better, but the city won't let them.

With the city website saying all fields won't be open until 2022, the vendors are rightfully concerned. The food is still worth the trek but with no games to watch or play in, there are far fewer people making the trip. Fancy cafes over on Clinton Street are also siphoning off potential neighborhood business, as are those Ikea meatballs and free Fairway samples.

On field 5, overgrown weeds occupy the space where first base used to sit. With the area so desolate, the remaining vendors seem almost like a forgotten tribe. You can smell the grilling meats and the corn tortillas before you even spot the trucks.

And as the trucks come into view, they cut a meager profile, the flags of their countries hang proudly out front, the picnic tables sparsely populated. The vendors are trying to get by until the day when the parks re-open and the lunch lines once again weave down the block. But they still don't know when that day will be.

Until that day comes, all the vendors can do is their best to stay open, feeding the families who live in the neighborhood and the few who still come to play. For the time being, they will still be setting up on Saturdays and Sundays, making favorites that have been in their families generations—pupusas, batidos, baleadas—and cooking up food that, for them, tastes like home.

Interview by Rebecca Bratburd
Photos by Christiann Koepke

Andy Ricker
POK POK, RED HOOK
40.68758° N, 74.00122° W

When Andy Ricker, the chef and owner of the Pok Pok empire, won the James Beard Award for Best Chef, Northwest in 2011, he said the foundation had "indirectly given the award to the chefs of Northern Thailand." Ricker replicates Northern Thai food with as much precision as possible at his restaurants in Portland, Brooklyn, and Los Angeles—but he's still a white guy from middle America. Yet when he flags a dish on one of his menus as "spicy," he means it.

Back in the early 1990s, in between stints as a cook in Portland, Ricker took odd jobs painting houses and playing in a punk band. Nothing resonated with him, until, on a whim, he visited a friend in Thailand and fell in love with the food and culture there. Since then, he has lived for months at a time in San Sai in the Chiang Mai province, immersing himself in the food and drinking culture.

After years of eating his way through the country, Ricker returned to the United States to open Pok Pok. It was 2005, Ricker was in his 40s, and the menu relied on roasted chicken and green papaya salad. Now he helms nine restaurants, and his not-yet-named second cookbook, about drinking culture in Thailand, is due out in fall of 2017.

We spoke to Ricker at his restaurant in the Red Hook section of Brooklyn, a quiet waterfront area with a strong artistic community and industrial charm, a neighborhood with tree-lined streets, brownstones, churches and parks that Ricker finds to be all-around "lovely." How did Ricker, an American from North Carolina, introduce a new generation of American diners to an expanded understanding of Thai cuisine, and frankly, nail the flavors?

—

You opened the first Pok Pok in Portland in 2005. When you were opening your next location in New York, why did you decide on Brooklyn?

One: the rent is cheap here. Five years ago, in Manhattan, the rent prices were already outrageous. We literally could not afford to open a large restaurant in Manhattan. We opened a tiny to-go spot on the Lower East Side that we kept for about three years, and then bounced out of it. Number two: We're able to do charcoal grilling out here. In New York City, you are allowed to grill outside if you're cooking at a restaurant. As long as you meet certain standards, it's totally on par with health code. The biggest problem is dealing with your neighbors, which, in Manhattan, makes this kind of operation basically impossible. There are too many people around, and you'd get complaints constantly. In Brooklyn, the population feels way less dense. Not to mention, getting a liquor license in Manhattan is a brawl. You either have to beg or you have to fight. Here, you can get a liquor license easily. And if you talk to restaurateurs, you'll know it's basically impossible to make a living in this business without a liquor license.

The third reason was personal: I like it out here. Brooklyn is more like Portland than Manhattan is, and I don't mean in the beard, suspenders, mustache, and $500 vest way. It has more of a community feeling. It's more spread out and laid-back than Manhattan. It felt homier to me. Also, there's a potential that this neighborhood holds—people actually need Thai food here, because this neighborhood is underserved.

How would you describe the food at Pok Pok?

We don't use the word "authenticity" here. We also don't use the word "traditional." Those words mean different things to different people. Instead, we use the term "specific regional" food.

What do you mean by that?

First of all, there's the context. This is a kind of restaurant that would exist in Thailand, basically. Number two: we use a lot of tools that you would use in a Thai kitchen. Mortar and pestle gets used all day, every day for a number of different recipes. The portion sizes are similar to what you would get in Thailand. The way the rice is served is how you would get it in Thailand. We make our minced meat with knives. We don't use grinders. It's hand-chopped every day. It's something we don't make a big deal about, but I bring knives that are specifically used for making laap [minced meat] back from Thailand, and we use those knives to chop the laap every day. The papaya salad gets made fresh with a mortar and pestle every time it's ordered. We do a lot of cooking on charcoal. We bring ingredients in from Thailand that you basically can't get here at all. We do dishes that rely on these ingredients. That's what I've built this restaurant on.

Pok Pok is trying to recreate something that exists somewhere else in a way that's understandable to Westerners. When I say that, I don't mean we dumb shit down, or we change things, or make things bigger. We just present it in a way that Westerners can generally understand. The descriptors on the menu are in English, and they're potentially over-descriptive, because most people don't have a frame of reference. If we did a shopping list menu, people would order the same shit they always do. The whole point of Pok Pok is to introduce people to things they may not have had before, and for it not to be scary for them.

Pok Pok is self-described as a "Northern Thai" restaurant. What are the regional differences in Thai food?

Northern Thailand is a specific region. Southern Thailand is a specific region. Central Thailand is the largest region. Each region has its own staple and its own relatively distinctive food culture. The various regions and their cuisines are defined by their geography, and the climate, and the ethnicity of the people who live there.

The staple in Southern Thailand is jasmine rice. The food there tends to be heavy on coconut cream and seafood because it's close to the ocean. It tends to be really, really spicy. There is a lot of influence from Malaysia, so a fair share of dry spice enters the kitchen.

Central Thailand is where Bangkok is, so you get royal cuisine. That's where a lot of the food you probably think of as Thai food comes from.

If you're talking about Isan food, or Lao food [in Northeastern Thailand], that's a different cuisine. The staple there is sticky rice. It tends to be very simple food. It is to Thailand what the food of the American South is to the United States.

Northern Thailand is mountainous: There are rivers, valleys, and jungles. It's landlocked. There's no access to the ocean, unless you travel great distances through Burma or Laos. There's not a whole lot of seafood there. There's freshwater fish, frog, wild game, and domestically raised animals like pig and chicken. Unlike most of the country, northerners eat quite a lot of beef. Most of the rest of the country doesn't eat much beef for many reasons, religion being one of them. The food tends to be herbaceous. There's a lot of boiled, steamed, and grilled food made from wild herbs and wild vegetables. Bitter flavors feature heavily.

What was it about Northern Thai food that sparked your obsession?

I happened to be in the right place at the right time. I was in Chiang Rai. I showed up at a particular time of year, and was taken to eat a particular local regional dish [Kaeng het thawp, a wild, puffed mushroom dish]. It was unlike anything I had ever had before. It was bitter, sour, herbaceous, soupy, and salty. It was really delicious and really surprising. It made me start to think, well, this is a local, regional dish that is seasonal. This means that this is probably true all over Thailand. What I've been eating at home obviously is a tiny sliver of dishes that have translated well to American menus. So, I wanted to know more.

You've said before that Thai people, like all people, experiment and deviate from traditional recipes. Are there any dishes you've modified for Pok Pok?

I don't give myself as much liberty to do that. When I opened this restaurant, I decided to try to accurately recreate what I saw there because I didn't think it needed altering. At the time, I didn't feel like I was qualified to alter anything because I didn't fully understand the food. I still don't fully understand the food. I won't ever be a master of this shit. The older I get, and the more I go there and study this stuff, the more I learn. At this point, if I wanted to start fucking with it, I could. But I don't want to, because my favorite restaurants in Thailand are the places where you go, and ten years later, you go again and it's exactly the same. I think there's a huge amount of respect and honor in doing the thing you do really, really well and just doing it forever. Never letting it get worse, and always trying to make it better somehow.

How do you sustain something like that?

It doesn't necessarily mean changing recipes drastically. It's finding better sources for the meat, getting fresher herbs, or finding new techniques that make a dish taste better, even marginally. The freedom that I have is that I'm not locked to any one genre, or any particular style of cooking, so I can put dishes on the menu that are a little bit around the map (of Thailand). I don't get bored doing this.

People are creatures of habit. They go to the same place to get the same dish, more often than they'll go out and eat adventurously. I know people who've been coming to this restaurant for five years and they order the same thing every time they walk in the door. I'm the same way. When I go to a diner that's been there for 30 years, I'm having the damn French toast. There are people that like to go out and try something new, but you're not going to do that every night. That's the nature of a neighborhood restaurant, especially a New York restaurant. It's built on people who are regulars.

We're not trying to get chef-y on things. I only get chef-y on things when we're doing a special event. I'll let my freak flag fly a little bit. Why fuck with something that is great as it is, especially when it's not even your own thing? When I was younger, I had a really chef-y ego. Everything had to be cool and new and I had to make it up. I basically gave up that side of the chef ego. It removes a lot of pressure. Running restaurants is an insanely difficult job, and not having to come up with a new fucking menu every three weeks is a massive amount of time and effort saved.

In ten years, what do you think the status Thai food in America will be? In Brooklyn?

I had no idea when I opened what it would be like in one year or five years. I still have no idea now. I have hopes. I hope that more Thai open specialty shops (a shop that specializes in typically one dish) as they do in Thailand. If you want to eat pad Thai, you go to the pad Thai shop. It doesn't have 50 other things on the menu.

Meanwhile, the vast majority of new Thai restaurants try to find a way to do fusion food or incorporate as much diversity as possible to draw in as many people as they can. But, thankfully, restaurants like Somtum Der in the East Village, which still doesn't have pad Thai on the menu, are specializing. The thrust of its menu is to serve Isan food. I hope a Southern Thai place opens up, because, in New York, that is the least represented, least understood, and least appreciated of all Thai regional cooking.

I also hope that people start doing their own thing. So far what's happened is, for instance, somebody in Portland—Nong [Poonsukwattana], who used to work for me—opened a khao man gai shop, and she became famous. Now there are three khao man gai places in New York. Instead of people saying, "Oh, cool, someone opened a khao man gai restaurant, so why don't I do boat noodles?" they're going, "I'm going to sell khao man gai, too."

All the Grocery Stores I've Known
By Kyle Chayka

My six years living in Brooklyn could be told as a series of grocery stores. Or, rather, bodegas, the traditional New York corner stores that play host to everything from itinerant cats to dusty boxes of off-brand mac-and-cheese.

When I first moved to Bushwick, the closest bodega to my apartment was Brooklyn Natural, an upscale general store abutting the subway. Twenty-four hours a day, I could stop into the neighborhood's de facto hitching post to buy bunches of bananas, fresh cups of only barely sludgy coffee, frozen dumplings, pre-made food, or packs of cigarettes. In the industrial-bucolic area, I often imagined the hipsters straggling in every morning as farmers on their way out to the fields (or in this case, their art studios) with tote bags instead of tools.

When I moved to Greenpoint, an old-school Polish neighborhood that has reached a profitable détente with its gentrifiers, I began frequenting Key Food. This location of the grocery chain took on a Polish tinge. It was easier to get chunks of bacon than the sliced kind, and so I frequently made meals of frozen pierogis and pasta with thick cubes of fatty pork, a less Italian version of pancetta. What I frequented most were the Korean-run produce stands and bodegas. The owners were friendlier than the perennially grumpy local oldsters. In their antiseptically well-lit aisles, it was possible to get organic gochujang and homemade kimchi, alongside my requisite hangover kombucha.

By the time I moved back to Bushwick a year later, a charcuterie store called Hops & Hocks opened just down the street from my apartment, with a hand-painted mural of a giant ham leg advertising its presence. Suddenly, an entire world of cured meat flooded Morgan Avenue, bringing prosciutto, salami, and pâté (not to mention locally made marshmallows and tap-filled growlers) to an area that didn't know what it was missing.

Its proximity to my apartment made me slightly too pleased with myself. I began bringing speck to every social gathering, inspiring a running joke among my friends. I was that Bushwick guy. And when a new coffee roaster, Supercrown, opened its minimalist headquarters just down the block, I couldn't stop bragging about it. If you can't have a distinctive Brooklyn brand of insufferable pride in your own neighborhood, where can you?

I live in East Williamsburg now, in an historically Italian area, dense with food, that spreads around the main street of Graham Avenue. The aptly named Emily's Pork Store on Graham sells any pig part you're looking for, and Anthony and Son Panini Shoppe will slice it into a classic sandwich. C-Town is the lifeline of the neighborhood, a storefront supermarket where young families wander through the labyrinthine shelves next to seniors picking up rotisserie chickens and to-go meals.

Brooklyn groceries follow trends with the alacrity of subway platform ads; the shelf stock changes weekly. New ingredients pop up in grocery stores and bodegas as certain foods go offline-viral. With the Ottolenghi deluge, a friend observed how C-Town started carrying ground lamb and za'atar. The new Whole Foods around here even stocks turmeric root and spiralized zucchini.

But if I'm being honest, lately I've become like most New Yorkers I know. My fridge is bare except for a few bottles of hot sauce. It's where my roommate keeps his batteries. I don't even order pantry staples from Amazon or Fresh Direct. Bodegas and specialty grocery stores are mostly vital for supplying last-minute snacks. Mostly, I eat out. Because the best part about living in Brooklyn is that having so many grocery stores around usually means there are even more restaurants.

Interview by Rebecca Bratburd

Okonomi

OKONOMI, WILLIAMSBURG
40.71253° N, 73.94878° W

Entering Okonomi, a tiny, 12-seat restaurant in Williamsburg, feels like walking into a friend's apartment. Focused, easy-going servers who feel more like new friends than wait staff tend to diners, quietly refilling small ceramic teacups. Much like eating at a friend's place, there is no menu. A set modeled after a traditional Japanese breakfast greets diners with seven-grain rice, miso soup, roasted fish, and pickled vegetables. It's one of the most intimate meals in Brooklyn.

But traditional Japanese breakfast in the hands of head chef JT Vuong leans more New York than Japan. It comes complete with brightly colored, seasonal vegetables fresh from the city's Greenmarket and fish caught in nearby waters, an extension of the restaurant's guiding philosophies of mottainai ("don't waste") and kansha ("gratitude"). Yuji Haraguchi, who owns Okonomi, is building his shape-shifting restaurant and new Japanese fish market on these Japanese principles, encouraging appreciation of ingredients and resourcefulness above all else.

Previously a seafood wholesaler in Japan's Utsunomiya-city, Haraguchi arrived in New York in 2009 to pursue his longtime dream of opening a restaurant. One year after opening, the shoebox-sized restaurant, located in a neighborhood saturated with restaurants, commands multi-hour lines for set meals at breakfast and lunch and ramen at night. Now Luke Davin, Haraguchi's first hire, will manage a newly opened Japanese-style fish market, Osakana ("honor your fish") that takes their dedication to sustainable fishing a step further. We spoke to Vuong and Davin to learn more.

How do you characterize your style of cooking?

Vuong: The essence is that everything is presented as a taste, in small portions. We adjust ingredients minimally. What we do requires so much attention to detail— a lot of pickling and marinating, part of a tradition of preservation.

How does Brooklyn's urban environment impact the ingredients you cook with?

Davin: New York is a coastal town by location, and yet we aren't coastal eaters. People will go down to the Jersey Shore to eat seafood as though they're not living in a city right next to the water. But the stuff that is shipped down to the Jersey Shore is actually lower quality seafood. It's not like it's getting caught right off the shore.

Vuong: We buy a lot of our veggies from the Greenmarket [farmers' market]. A lot of that is local, from New Jersey, upstate New York, Connecticut, and Massachusetts. A lot of seafood comes from Maine and Canada. It's regional, though not necessarily local. We're not going to the backyard or down the street.

Davin: The Bluefish is very local, though. We're sourcing it from the Atlantic—ideally line-caught by American fishermen. It's not always hyper local but it is regional, because it's the kind of fish that naturally migrate through here.

Vuong: Tuna travel so much; I can tell you where ours was caught, but I can't tell you where it roamed.

Why open the fish market, Osakana, then? Does Brooklyn need a Japanese style fish market right now? And how is it going to be different from existing fish markets in New York?

Davin: The biggest differences will be with sanitation and handling. It's not that Brooklyn needs a fish market with a Japanese bent, but nowhere in New York is there a fish market taking Japanese care in cleaning. If you're looking to buy food to use for Japanese cuisine, there's not a single shop held to Japanese standards, mostly because it's not within the culture of what we expect a fish market to be here.

What do you mean by that?

Davin: There won't be piles of ice with piles of fish oxidizing on top. That's what we're trying to avoid: fish open to air where only a thin layer of fish pressed against the ice is at the right temperature, even though it's being crushed by whatever fish is on top of it. The fish at the top is drying out and oxidizing. All the while, the fish are going through the natural process of aging and spoilage. Existing markets promote the act of spoilage [by negligence] all the way down.

How does the Japanese cleaning method help prevent this?

Davin: We clean the surface of the fish, removing the guts and the head. From there, the torso is as clean as possible and intact, regulating its own moisture levels. We rinse the fish thoroughly, then take the scales off with a tool called an urokotori that has small flat teeth that get just under the scales and lift them away. After all the scales are clear, we rinse the fish again and wipe the skin clean and dry before we ever cut into the fish. This treatment is very important for sashimi, because contaminants from the outside of the fish can be carried to the meat inside by your knife if you don't clean the fish thoroughly first. I also clean my knife as I'm fileting the fish so that the meat is pristine when presented for sashimi. Fish is so delicate; it bruises. Sometimes people think they're bad at working with fish, but it's actually that the people who handled the fish before them handled it poorly and set them up for failure.

Vuong: Water leaches out of the fish during handling, which makes the fish seem less fresh by the time it's served. People come to Okonomi and ask why our fish tastes so fresh. We haven't done anything to it.

Davin: It's more about not doing certain things: not leaving it on a pile of ice, not letting it come to temperature, not letting it oxidize, which is especially important with fish like Spanish mackerel and Bluefish. They're so delicious because they're so rich in Omega-3 fatty oils. Oil goes rancid as it spoils—fish oil in particular, which is that "fishy" flavor so many people worry about. That's actually a sign of poor handling.

What will the buying experience be like at Osakana?

Davin: We'll most likely butcher to order. We'll see how much we have and how much we'll need to butcher ahead of time. We also want to offer an omakase ("chef's choice") box for customers who trust our methods and want to explore a couple of different kinds of fish. It will also be a way for us to manage inventory, too. Maybe people don't know what Porgy fish or Hog Snapper is. Hog Snapper has a terrible name and suffers from poor branding, but it is one of the most delicious fish I've ever eaten. Hog snapper eat a lot of shrimp, so the meat has a shrimpy sweetness. We'd like to offer a Hog Snapper with maybe a Spanish mackerel as part of the omakase box, along with other fish people are familiar with.

Is there an educational aspect to the store?

Davin: Yes, there will be butchery demos every day. And we want to have basic Japanese knife care available on an open demo basis. We want to do more hands-on classes, to the point where you're coming into the kitchen and being tutored in small groups. Those are down the road. We want to carry products essential to basic Japanese home cooking, including bonito and dashi. Japanese food is based on foundational ingredients, ratios, and techniques. Those techniques can be used on anything you buy at the farmers' market.

Vuong: It's about care, basically. That's the overarching philosophy.

Davin: We want you to want to use the whole fish. We want customers to know how to use the head and the bones. Ramen is what we use it for here. Fish isn't even usually used for ramen. There's so much you can do with fish stock.

What's your approach to plating? Everything seems so precise at Okonomi.

Vuong: Plating is important. If one thing is slightly off, just one or two centimeters off-center, it looks bad. Apparently in Western culture, the rule of three applies [i.e., the rule of odds commonly used in photography and the arts]. Everything is served in three pieces, so there's still a chance for symmetry.

Do you follow that rule of three?

Davin: As long as it's not four. One of the pronunciations for "four" in Japanese is the same as "death." In the U.S., we don't have 13th floors in hospitals; in Japan, they don't have fourth floors in hospitals. You never want to put four pieces of radishes in a bowl of soup, as ridiculous as that seems.

What's your favorite task in the kitchen?

Davin: Scaling tilefish. It's such a delicate process. You're cutting between the skin, so there are scales and a thin layer of webbing that holds the scales. That webbing is a lot of times where the color comes from. Any little twist of the wrist can cut into the skin and leave a mark. When you're preparing tilefish for sashimi, those little marks are a really noticeable imperfection. It's very satisfying once you learn how to do it right.

Vuong: I like grinding the sesame seeds after they've been roasted for our tofu dressing. When you grind the seeds, about a cup at a time, an intoxicating aroma is released.

What do you cook at home, when you're not working at the restaurant?

Vuong: I don't eat seafood at home, because, for one thing, it's hard to get the same quality of fish that we get at the restaurant and, for another, I eat so much fish while I'm here. I eat a lot of poultry at home. I play a lot with shio koji, a rice ball that's used to make soy sauce, miso, and a bunch of other things. It breaks down proteins really well. I've been putting it on any kind of protein I can find. It makes it a bit sweeter and saltier. I sauté veggies at home because, at the restaurant, we blanch almost everything.

Davin: American or Eastern European comfort food for me. My grandmother worked in restaurants as a short-order cook in Pennsylvania. I keep a quart of salsa at home and I always have refried beans on hand. I like Filipino adobo pork; it keeps really well. I like chicken thighs because there's nothing you can't make out of chicken thighs. But my last meal would be buttermilk biscuits and sausage gravy with a poached egg on top.

Brooklyn's Spirit
by Andrew Scheinman

"Whiskey has always depended on storytelling," says Colin Spoelman, co-founder and lead distiller of Brooklyn's Kings County Distillery. "Which can exist in any era."

American mythology would have you believe that distilleries flourish only in rural Kentucky and Tennessee, nestled into rolling bluegrass hills by legends such as Jim Beam and Jack Daniels. Spoelman, a native Kentuckian who wrote the book *Dead Distillers* about just this sort of lore, aims to expand that story and exhume his adopted borough's distilling tradition to usher in a new era of spirits in Brooklyn.

The first distillery in the United States, as it turns out, was opened on Staten Island by the Dutch in 1640, birthing a New York industry that, until the Civil War, would produce more liquor than Maryland, Pennsylvania, Kentucky, and Tennessee combined. In the colonial era, Dutch and British settlers produced rum from Caribbean molasses—an amalgamation of culture that would presage the New York melting pot to come. But when the War of 1812 cut foreign supply, producers switched to locally available rye and made whiskey instead. Bolstered over the following few decades by Scots-Irish immigrants and their ancestral expertise, New York City's whiskey business succumbed to the industrial urban growth of a reunited country. The nail in the coffin came some half-century later, with Prohibition famously slashing production. While all distilleries—urban and rural—were shut down, city-based operations were too expensive to reopen due to the growing cost of real estate. Distillers holed away in the countryside, and Brooklyn was definitely not that pasture.

It was actually not until 2007, with the passage of the New York Farm Distillery Law, that urban distilleries became profitable in the city again. Championed in large part by Ralph Erenzo—founder of the first distillery in the state of this new wave, Tuthilltown Spirits in the Hudson Valley—the law authorizes the operation of small distilleries that source at least half of their crop from in-state. With a growing locavore movement in the borough and the proliferation of small distilleries nationwide, Brooklynites took notice.

Native Kentuckian Colin Spoelman was one of these Brooklynites. A hobbyist who tinkered his way into the bourbon industry, Spoelman built Kings County in 2010 from an informal moonshine operation popular among his friends back home. Living locally, Spoelman set up shop nearby in a tiny East Williamsburg room, at the time the smallest commercial distillery in the country. But whiskey requires stories and nostalgia, and in New York, long considered rye country, Spoelman mined the past to justify making corn whiskey. Unearthing centuries of spirits tales, he became something of a historian, writing books and establishing the Boozeum—a museum of New York distilling history—alongside Kings County's new operation in the landmark Paymaster Building at the Brooklyn Navy Yard. Retroactively legitimizing this Brooklyn distilling history in a museum helped the young business grow, making nearly 400 years of the whiskey's story available next door to where the product is being sold. Kings County's distilling process mirrors this historical overlay: Old Scots-Irish and Kentuckian techniques meet homegrown New York grains and partnering with Brooklyn's Mast Brothers chocolate yields an array of corn whiskeys that intentionally combine new and old.

Like Kings County, New York Distilling Company (NYDC) was devised with a zealous approach to historical excavation, billing itself with the tagline, "A return to distilling in Brooklyn," at its Williamsburg location. Founded in 2011 by Brooklyn Brewery cofounder Tom Potter, his son, Bill Potter, and Allen Katz of Southern Wine & Spirits, NYDC pushes its roots even deeper than its peers, exhuming a particular New York story with each product. Its Perry's Tot - Navy Strength Gin, for example, is named for Commandant Matthew Perry of the Brooklyn Navy Yard and alludes to the borough's gritty naval history. Distilled to 57 percent alcohol by volume, it would allegedly not soil gunpowder if spilled. Mister Katz's Rock & Rye looks

to 19th century saloons, reimagining an old-school tonic made of young rye, rock candy sugar, and sour cherries to conjure images of chewing tobacco and corner drugstores. Further still, Chief Gowanus New Netherlands Gin, created with Brooklyn booze historian David Wondrich, is based on a centuries-old "Holland gin" recipe from the Dutch days.

Yet this historical bent ignores hundreds of years of change and development. Take, for instance, the fact that Brooklyn and New York City were two separate cities until 1898; their complete merger took place entirely within this timeframe. More than one tumultuous century later, Brooklyn is radically diverse, its neighborhoods defined by the countless population shifts of immigration, architectural decay, and gentrification.

Other new distilleries have leaned into this present-day reality, building their brands on a celebration of the more recent global diaspora. Jack from Brooklyn and Cacao Prieto, two distilleries located in Red Hook, take cues from the Caribbean, for example. Jack produces Sorel, a sweetened hibiscus, ginger, nutmeg, cassia, and clove infusion inspired by Jamaican and Trinidadian traditions, while chocolatier Cacao Prieto makes an eponymous aged brandy from fermented Dominican cacao alongside its bean-to-bar chocolate. Not quite steeped in centuries of Brooklyn distilling folklore, these producers embody a new kind of local, one that superimposes faraway traditions on the borough and embraces its residents' diverse origins.

What lies at the heart of this new crop of Brooklyn spirits is the continual adaptation and comingling of traditions new and old, near and far. They represent, in essence, the story of the constantly changing population of New York City's most populous borough—simultaneously drawing from local innovation and international influence. Nevertheless, this generation of distillers is young, with room to develop and refashion itself into a full cross-section of its 21st century Brooklyn. "Nothing is to stop New York distillers from coming together to try to articulate a regional style, based in history, but with contemporary interpretation," says Spoelman. "Sounds like a good idea, right?"

Perhaps, but it just may be that the truest definition of a Brooklyn spirit is its inability to be defined.

Interview by Maggie Spicer

Jeppe Jarnit-Bjergsø
TØRST / LUKSUS, GREENPOINT
40.72344° N, 73.95077° W

Danish brewer Jeppe Jarnit-Bjergso moved to the United States in 2012 intent on opening one of the world's best beer bars. That bar, Tørst, which means "thirst" in Danish, now sits behind an unmarked white facade on Greenpoint's Manhattan Avenue. Together with Noma and Momofuku test kitchen alum, Daniel Burns, he's conceived a space that's at once a blast from the past, right at home in present-day, gentrified Greenpoint, and a glimpse of the future of post-hipster Brooklyn, where liking what you like isn't an ironic statement. Warm, unfinished wood-clad walls are tempered by the clean lines of a gleaming bar, an altar to 21 taps, and the perfect showcase for the renowned brewery Evil Twin, which Jarnit-Bjergso founded as a home-brewer back in Denmark. Pair that with the Michelin-starred restaurant—Luksus, inspired by an extra stove he found in the space when he signed the lease—tucked behind a secret wall in the back, and you know Jarnit-Bjergso's done it: He has endowed New York with a destination bar, a low-lit beer sanctuary uniquely equipped to meet the demands of Brooklyn as we know it now.

What is the New York beer scene like?

Exploding. It's growing like crazy. But it wasn't always this way. When I moved to New York in 2012, I think New York was a little behind the rest of the country. Breweries and beer bars were opening up everywhere, but NYC didn't have that much going on. The beer bar scene was lagging behind. After we opened Tørst, so many new breweries opened.

Why do you think that's the case?

I think the main reason is real estate. It's so expensive; you have to have a good business plan. It's a little riskier in New York, but now you're hearing about new breweries opening weekly, it seems. In fact, there's a new brewery opening five minutes away from us. It's a good thing. More beer people will come to New York if there are more places to go.

How did you become interested in beer?

As a young guy back in Denmark becoming a teacher, I was going out and drinking beer, but I found it kind of boring. You'd just be drinking Carlsberg [arguably the Budweiser of Denmark] products and imports. There wasn't really a "wow" moment. I just had a desire to try something different. I've always been into food and exploring different flavors, so I started a beer club. It was 1998. I wanted something more interesting than Carlsberg as the only option. I invited 15 friends. Everyone brought a different beer. We'd do a blind tasting, talk about the beer, and rate them. We started going to bodegas (Danish for dive bar) as a group to drink porters. I began discovering beer that was so different from the bland lagers I was used to. It was then that I realized how diverse and interesting beer could be, and just how much more there was to explore.

In a way, that led to my first adventure in the beer business. In 2005, I opened the beer shop Ølbutikken in Copenhagen. I was done with teaching school, and was getting more and more into beer and home brewing. It was a simple decision—I couldn't get the beers I wanted so I opened a shop. I'm very pragmatic in that sense.

Why beer?

It's kind of a coincidence. Looking back it could have been something else—spirits, for example. But beer was more approachable when I was a poor student. Had I been able to afford good wines back then, who knows? Maybe I would have made wine. I've been into a lot of different things. I used to sell mid-century furniture.

I got into beer because I wanted to explore different flavors.

Tell us about Evil Twin.

Evil Twin began in 2010. I was still a teacher at the time. I was home brewing and had the shop. It became a fun project for me to make beer, so I started Evil Twin. I never meant for it to be anything serious. I definitely did not have a business plan. I just wanted to brew a few beers, sell them, and see if people liked them. I started getting really great responses, so I adapted my home-brewing recipes to a larger scale. It just made sense to start selling to bars and shops in Copenhagen.

What brought you to New York, and how did you become a beer producer?

I met a guy at the end of 2010 who had an import business in New York. He'd heard about me. He said, "If you ever want to send Evil Twin to the United States, I will gladly take it." So I sent him the first batch and it all sold in one day. I was traveling to Spain, Holland, and

Norway regularly at the time to brew all these beers as the business scaled, since I couldn't find the capacity I needed to keep the brewing in Denmark. We'd gotten a couple opportunities to start brewing in the U.S., so I moved to the States in 2012 to grow and develop the brand. I know it's cliche to say, but if you can make it here, you can make it anywhere, so I decided to try it out. I started to feel the hype pretty quickly once we opened Tørst and Luksus, with the media saying that we were changing the beer scene in New York. I definitely began to feel I had set my footprint on the city.

What inspired Tørst?

Two things. First: It was to have a place where we could go hang out with our friends. Second: I wanted to create something unique. I'm the kind of guy where if nobody else does it, I just do it myself. Tørst is not just another beer bar, and it didn't just become supposedly one of the best beer bars in the world. We created it to be the best, and we worked very hard for it to become what it is. That was our purpose from the very beginning. If I'm not among the best, I'm not going to do it. I used to play soccer, and I sucked at it; I quit because I didn't want to do something I wasn't good at. For me competition is the best thing that can happen, because it makes me better at what I do.

How does Tørst fit into Brooklyn?

When we opened a small 16-seat restaurant in the back of the bar in an unknown part of Brooklyn, it was ballsy and risky. But I think that's a Brooklyn thing. You don't see that in Manhattan; you don't see it in many other places. Brooklyn places are craftier, artsier, and feel more real and unique than Manhattan places do. That's what I love about Brooklyn. It's about finding things yourself. We don't even have a sign for the bar. It's very small and you have to put your head right in front. The whole idea was to create a Brooklyn feel. It's Denmark meets Brooklyn. It's the curiosity to go and explore; you wouldn't have that in Manhattan where it's more about glam and pretentiousness. It's important that we made it approachable because you want people to come in and feel welcome, not that it's a show.

What distinguishes Tørst from other beer bars?

We don't compromise whatsoever. I think that's what makes us stand out. There are a lot of people who say they don't compromise but it's not true. Watching the beer bar scene around New York and the rest of the country, I often see people taking in what they're offered by some sales rep. If there's a new big brewery that comes into town, it seems like everyone is doing a tap for that brewery. At Tørst, if we don't believe in it, we don't take it in. Sure, we could sell more beer and make more money by compromising a little bit. Our staff is all crazy beer nerds and all home brewers who are very knowledgeable. You can see that when you come in. Also, our draft system is the most high tech ever made. I learned about it when I was visiting a friend in California who built the system. If it makes the serving better, and you know it exists, how can you not have it? It's about bringing out the best flavors.

Tell me about Luksus. What's the relationship to Tørst?

When we found the space for Tørst, it had a kitchen, so one day I got this idea: Why don't we open a restaurant? I want people to come into a beer bar because beer is what we do, but then we happen to have a secret restaurant in the back. I kind of like the twist on it. We were part of Gelinaz in Copenhagen years ago. All of the chefs either had been to or owned the best places, and they all came in to eat and were fascinated by a secret restaurant in the back of a beer bar. It made me realize that what we do is very unique.

Why open in Greenpoint?

Greenpoint reminds me a little of Copenhagen, a little like home. I like to go to Manhattan for half a day but otherwise it's too much. My importer Brian lives in Brooklyn, and when I started traveling here, I always stayed at his place. Brooklyn's quiet and has more of a local feel to it. People say hello to each other on the street. Williamsburg was already a little bit over-saturated, and Greenpoint just seemed cool and happening, and up-and-coming. We got in four years ago. It looked very different then. For us, it was more fun to move into an area and be able to change it a little than to move into an area already happening. When we got the lease in 2012, it was $60 per square foot. Now the store down the street from us is $120 per square foot. There's no way you can run a business on Bedford. It's sad; it pushes out all the real businesses. No one can open a small cheese shop and pay $250 per square foot. Maybe Whole Foods.

Would Tørst be possible in another borough?

The "concept" of Tørst, in my opinion, is so unique that it would fit in anywhere and would make an impact anywhere. I know it's seen as "high end" for beer bars, but I think that's what the world needs now. There are so many of the same places out there. It's time to show what beer really is and I think that's what we do well. We could open a Tørst and it would be successful no matter where in the world we did it.

What is high-end beer?

That's up to the drinker to decide. What is high-end wine? Probably just wine that costs more. Craft, expensive, well-made—I think it's hard to determine what exactly high-end beer is. Pretty much every beer in this world, even Bud, is made from the same ingredients. That's what I found fascinating about brewing—we all have the same starting point but get different results. Unlike wine, which is terroir-based, beer is nearly all recipe-based. That's what I love about it. You can make the best beer in the world at home in your kitchen. If you wanted to start a winery today, you can't just get the best soil, sunshine, or vineyards. You have to wait 100 years before you can start making good wine. With beer, you can go down to the corner store and buy hops and wheat then go home and make beer. That—to me—is fascinating.

Why 21 taps?

I always had this number in mind. Seven light beers, seven medium, and seven strong or dark. It's just a good number. You have to compromise if you have 100 taps. The beers aren't fresh. Around one third of the beer served at Tørst is Evil Twin.

How do you feel about New Nordic as a trend?

I think it's great obviously, and it's also helped us a lot because we got attention when we moved over. Being from Denmark, I am extremely proud of René [Redzepi] and Noma, and what he's achieved for Denmark. You could almost say he's made it easier for the rest of us. I think the New Nordic thing has become a little bit cliché, and I think misused a little bit by some. It was important for us to go out and say we're not doing New Nordic, because how can you do that in New York? I don't think it's possible because it's so much about the ingredients. Sure, there are the same techniques and style of food but it's not New Nordic in that sense. I love when René said in the documentary, "New Nordic is dead." It's definitely overdone. But it also helped all of us a lot.

What was it like to work with Noma?

I was eating at Noma one time and the sommelier came down and asked if I wanted to see the beer list. I said, "Honestly I don't think it's very good. I think it's very generic. People come to Noma to get a special experience and I don't think the beer list is representative." They said to me, "Maybe you can do it better?" So I said, "Yeah, let me give it a try." At the time they had 40-50 beers on the menu. We talked about cutting the list down to five different beers created for Noma. Brewers making specific beers that included ingredients they actually use on the menu was an obvious thing. Evil Twin did a Noma juniper and Noma oxalis [wood sorrel] beer, and the remaining three were made by other Danish breweries.

You've been after the unofficial title for the world's best beer bar. Do you feel you've achieved it?

I'd like to think we have. I'm not very Danish in that sense. But, when I do something, I'm extremely competitive and want to be the best at what I do. In the last three years I haven't seen one list of "The World's Best Beer Bars" that we haven't been on. Am I saying there are no beer bars out there that can match? No, there are beer bars in Europe that have a better beer selection; there are a lot of restrictions in New York, and we just can't get those beers. From what we have to work with, I don't think you can make a better beer bar.

What's on the horizon?

We're building a brewery in Brooklyn, off the Halsey stop. It will open before next summer. Evil Twin has always been the main business. It's the one I spend the most time on. Sometimes more people ask about Tørst because they can see it and experience it. With Evil Twin, it's harder to relate because you can't really come and visit us. We've become known, but to become a local New York brand, we need to have a space people can visit, and we're growing so much right now. By opening the brewery, we can get better at what we do.

Finally: Brooklyn Fare
By Matt Mark

When people ask me about the Chef's Table at Brooklyn Fare, all I can think about is the four-year journey it took for me to get there. One of my friends, who lives in New York, recommended it to my wife Gizelle and me in early 2011. But each of the two times we visited New York that year, the restaurant was already fully booked or closed.

Back home in Toronto, where I spend my free time online talking about and filming whiskey, I would continue to see Brooklyn Fare featured in "Top Restaurant" lists or praised in online posts about the restaurant. I realized that we would have to really dedicate ourselves to scoring a reservation if we were to succeed. Even then, we missed opportunities to eat there twice in 2012 (waitlisted), once in 2013 (closed), and again in 2014 (waitlisted).

But I knew we would be going to New York over Labor Day weekend in 2015, and I was determined to get in.

I missed out on a slot for the early part of our trip, but the following week, I was able to secure a reservation for four after redialing approximately 100 times. Commitment paid off.

Many people we knew opted out of eating at Brooklyn Fare because of its "No Photo/Notes" policy, deeming it too restrictive. So many of our friends who work in the food business derive pleasure not only from eating out, but also from writing, photographing, and posting about their experiences. But that same friend from New York (who frequents many of the city's fine dining restaurants) told us that he considered Brooklyn Fare to be one of his favorite places, so we only grew more excited.

I can't imagine what the informal dining experience was previously like in the actual Brooklyn Fare grocery store. The space previously had a table located beside a small kitchen. I imagined it to be a very crowded and cramped Dean and Deluca with a simple kitchenette in the back. It was about $70 for seven courses in 2009. These days, it's more like $300 for 15 to 20 courses.

When you walk into the new kitchen, which is located in the building adjacent to the store, there is seating for up to 18 diners. The counter is arranged in a D-shape and connected to an open kitchen, where Ramirez puts the final touches on dishes while his team of cooks preps fish, meat, and vegetables with exacting precision. Stainless steel workstations and a communal table give it all a clean and efficient look, like you've entered the guts of a well-oiled machine cranking at full speed. Built-in wine fridges and copper-lined pots that hang from a ceiling rack complete the look.

We were booked for the early timeslot at 7 pm; all seats were full. Once everyone was seated and wine orders were placed with the friendly, lone server, we settled into the communal experience. Everyone sat in close quarters. The mood was formal and quiet.

While the audience dines, quietly and on best behavior, Chef Ramirez and his team are in constant motion, delivering one course then transitioning to the next with ease. Starter bites included a refreshing, briny trout roe tartlet followed by Osetra caviar on sturgeon cream and Hokkaido uni on toast with black truffle. There was a focus on seafood, but the arc of the meal bent toward meat at the end and included A5 wagyu beef with daikon, foie gras soup, and duck breast.

There were only small breaks of a few reverent minutes between dishes. Diners quietly made sounds of delight— audible "mmm"s & "ahhs" cutting through the relative silence—and conversations about the dishes ensued in hushed tones. Most diners were in pairs, whispering to each other about the chef's discerning dedication to importing the highest quality ingredients from all over the world. *Did you know he flew in the fish from Japan?*

Most other spots that I've visited in Brooklyn, such as Pok Pok and Roberta's, are casual, chaotic, and busy. The borough has a dearth of formal and long-format (where 20 or more dishes are deftly produced by a very small kitchen team) dining. The two restaurants that bring this tradition to the borough are Blanca and Brooklyn Fare, neither of which require jackets. But, where Blanca, owned by the chef of Roberta's, is more rock and roll, Brooklyn Fare is a Zen garden.

I always look forward to eating in New York, especially in Brooklyn, which is home to some of the greatest dining diversity in the United States, and also some of the best fine dining. But there was a moment during the meal, when I looked at my wife and quietly noted that some dishes reminded me of a meal earlier in the spring of 2015, at Saison in San Francisco. The seafood focus was a logical connection point, but I was taken more by the caviar and uni dishes. Even in this supposedly singular experience, it was as if I had seen and eaten them before on a different coast, prepared by different chefs at a different time.

It wasn't the first time I felt this way, and it surely won't be the last. At this high a price and recognition level, it's possible I apply a different level of comparison and scrutiny. Mostly I wonder, are the similarities a logical result of chefs riffing on the classics? Or, even with a restriction on circulating images from Brooklyn Fare, is there just a general convergence in fine dining as a result of social media and sharing? Does it even matter?

Yet in fine dining, where the overall experience can be as influential as the food, Brooklyn Fare did not disappoint. I finally ate there—and it was one of the best meals I had all year.

Brooklyn Generic
By Kyle Chayka

Here's a dining problem you can only have in the 21st century, and really only in places like Brooklyn. A friend posts an Instagram photo from a bar. It looks like a place around the corner from your apartment—a local spot with burnished wood, minimalist metal stools, and Edison bulbs in wrought-iron cages. Without the geotag, you would never know, because every cafe, dive, and restaurant looks remarkably the same, down to the supposedly one-of-a-kind, salvaged coffee table. The aesthetic is Brooklyn Generic, and it's everywhere.

The word generic comes from the Latin for race or kind. By the 17th century, it expressed belonging to a large group of objects, a meaning made more relevant in the age of mass manufacturing. It's true that Brooklyn Generic has become a mass-manufactured aesthetic. It replicates itself endlessly, until we're as tired of it as we once were of Victorian chintz or shag rugs. But the more abstract significance of the word is also important, because it also suggests being part of a community.

Brooklyn Generic emerged from a combination of hipster style (i.e., heritage and artisanal), Steampunk's mixture of technology and organic materials, and the Depression-era nostalgia incited by the 2008 financial crisis. It has become the default style of cultural creative types not just in New York but all over the world. You can see it on Instagram, when your friends post that photo of a copycat bar, or you can see it for yourself: Just wander around any city and stop into the first place that has a cluster of twenty-somethings waiting outside on a Sunday morning. You'll see expanses of reclaimed wood, maybe some polished copper accents, and succulents in small ceramic pots dotting the interior. It's an eerie homogeneity: You never know quite where you are.

Familiarity with the style creates a level of comfort for those who recognize it. The distinctive aesthetic signals that you've ended up in a place belonging to a global monoculture, a sort of transnational hipster circuit. Brooklyn Generic has been replicated so many times that it's less about a specific place than the people who identify with it, whether in Beijing, Bangkok, or Belgrade. It's also about a certain set of shared values: the love of local food, good drink, and the chance to come together with a community over both.

I moved to Brooklyn in 2010, not quite at the beginning of the borough's march toward international fame as the home of hipsterdom, but somewhere towards its middle, just before its peak in popularity in 2011 and 2012. I first lived off the Morgan L subway stop, farther down the line that forms hipster Brooklyn's umbilical cord to Manhattan through Williamsburg. I lived in "Morgantown," an area of decrepit industrial warehouses that was home to artist studios and a few remaining manufacturing companies. It's also the birthplace of Roberta's, a restaurant that has been the most influential in propagating Brooklyn Generic.

Roberta's opened in 2008 on a side street in that part of Bushwick as a hidden spot with a cinderblock facade that didn't look like much until you passed through the door. Once inside, it resembled a hunting lodge, if only the prey were pizza. The space is full of dark wood, from the tables to the ceiling beams, and it conveyed an industrial chic that is of a piece with its neighborhood. Behind the restaurant, Roberta's extended into a series of refurbished storage containers that held eating and drinking areas as well as an independent radio broadcast studio.

Roberta's has never been less than relevant, even as it ages into its second decade. Its employees have gone on to start what often seems like most of the new restaurants in Brooklyn (at least the ones that get rabid media coverage), and its aesthetic quickly became equally influential. But it took another restaurant opening in 2008, however, to truly codify the look.

Five Leaves, a gastropub on the border of Williamsburg and Greenpoint, opened in September of 2008, and it hasn't stopped being busy since. The interior is what a Parisian cafe might be if you opened one in Depression-era New York: marble

countertops set against crowded stools, small tables wedged together, metal accents everywhere, a general feeling of comfortable clutter, but still clean. It's old, new, and everything in between.

It was designed by a man named John McCormick, the unsung hero of Brooklyn Generic. He's behind a bevy of Brooklyn restaurants, from the beer garden Spritzenhaus to the oyster house Maison Premiere. He's the one behind all of those seemingly rustic, salvaged antiques and pockmarked wood, the one creating the feeling that you've been transported in time but also remain perfectly in the present. "I'm a classicist when it comes to restaurants and bars," he said in an interview with Brooklyn Magazine, focusing on a few materials like marble and hardwood in order to inspire an "appreciation of New York history, trying to find these old places and reintroduce the aesthetic and the things that were kind of lost."

There's a value to timeless spaces in which we feel completely at home even though they're not of a particular era or place. It might be confusing on social media, but the spread of this style isn't always a negative, or even boring, thing. When we step into a place that has interiors of the kind McCormick designs, it's a familiar experience: we know what to expect. Especially for city-dwellers, these spaces offer a ready-made collective living room, except we don't have to design them ourselves. We simply have to relax.

This style has been dominant in New York for the better part of a decade, with each restaurant telegraphing its diners' values through distinctive aesthetic details. For its noodle bar, Momofuku, located in Manhattan's East Village, chose an interior of polished blond wood. The décor of its sister restaurant, Momofuku's Ssäm Bar (opened in 2006 and currently under renovation), partakes of Roberta's dim coziness. San Francisco's Blue Bottle has expanded in locations across New York with an industrial-refurbished aesthetic that reveres the experience of getting coffee as much as drinking it. Here, customers can retreat into workaday, blue collar labor fantasies, as they check Facebook with the assembly line sameness and efficiency of a factory job.

My favorite new restaurant in Brooklyn, for both food and aesthetics, is Faro. The Italian-leaning pasta purveyor manages to adapt some of the touches of the Brooklyn Generic to a new vernacular, which is probably why I enjoy being there so much. The airy space has minimalist furniture and an industrial blankness, conveying that certain globalized identity, but it restores a kind of Hollywood glamour to the equation: not vintage but new. In the back of the space, open steel counters are stacked with handmade ceramic plates, each one unique.

A five-minute walk away, there's a new bar, Honey's, which serves mead that it brews in-house. The style is Brutalist, if it were under the influence of hipster witch covens. Concrete features heavily, but so do eerie geometric shapes and breezeblocks (cement bricks with elegant-looking holes drilled through them). It's more Sedona than Manhattan. Like so many young people in Brooklyn, the style is drifting toward Los Angeles, where the self-conscious decorating schemes at restaurants such as Sqirl exhibit a sensual spareness. This aesthetic appears to be the successor to the previous style, just as the center of influence seems to have shifted from Brooklyn to Los Angeles. Our old borough couldn't stay cool forever.

It could be that people are now more focused on health than rehashing comfort food, or maybe we, as citizens of the global generic want to make our physical spaces resemble the blank white backgrounds of the Internet. For whatever reason, Los Angeles seems to be the new cultural creative center. With this bicoastal ping-ponging, we're likely to see more spaces that look like California in New York. I don't mind this evolution; it's not good or bad. It just is. Taste always changes.

Either way, Brooklyn Generic has become synonymous with a specific "good" restaurant culturel: an emphasis on small plates, an acceptance of gruff service, a lack of reservations. In our current decade, it endows a space with an aura of cultural relevance, irreverence, and a standard of quality, in Brooklyn or abroad.

As I write this, I'm sitting in the new Whole Foods in Gowanus, Brooklyn, a sprawling palace of produce and pre-packaged products including frozen Roberta's pizzas—translating some of the artisanal obsessions of early-2000s Brooklyn for the mass market. On the roof is a restaurant and cafeteria space that looks out onto the low skyline. It features exposed brick, loft-style windows, and rough-hewn wood paneling. It's comfortable as well as efficient, and customers use it as much for dining as a community space. Grown-ups work freelance, wired into a sprawling laptop armada, while children run around the floor. Brooklyn Generic has successfully evolved into a wholly mainstream success.

Rather than being just about a neighborhood, about exclusivity in an expensive city, Brooklyn Generic is about a shared set of concerns and desires. It might be easy to reject Edison bulbs and reclaimed wood as overdone (at this point, they should probably be banned for a few decades until they reemerge as retro). But it's harder to disagree with the values behind the style — of stability, authenticity, and connection to your city and the people around you. The trick is being able to discern when a space is embracing a style along with the meaning it carries, or just being superficial—which is everything the style was against in the first place.

Pam Yung & José Ramírez-Ruiz

SEMILLA, WILLIAMSBURG
40.71145° N, 173.95785° W

Sitting close to the action is the only option at Semilla, a restaurant where guests filling only 18 seats at a U-shaped bar come for a tasting menu but leave banker habits of foie gras and caviar behind. Chefs Jose Ramírez-Ruiz and Pamela Yung knew there would be some head scratches from guests once they realized that the restaurant focuses on vegetables, enhanced with animal fat and served with house-made, crusty country loaves. But they came into the New York restaurant business at a time when young chefs with devil-may-care attitudes left Manhattan behind. Now, Semilla is ground zero for a new vegetable-focused style of cooking, where even the most skeptical diners leave believers, both in the duo's cooking and the borough in which they cook.

When did you move to New York?

José Ramírez-Ruiz: I moved to New York City around Christmas in 2006. I have lived in Williamsburg and Bushwick for the entire 10 years that I've lived here. I've witnessed the change that has happened in the neighborhood, but I'm one of the gentrifiers too.

What were those neighborhoods like when you first came here?

Ramírez: It was cheap and full of young people. The art community was crazy, and there was this really awesome energy. The beauty was that there was this local crowd of people—many of them were artists—who just lived in the neighborhood and worked in the neighborhood. Others were cooks that would commute to Manhattan. It was just a feeling. Half of the condos that are in Williamsburg right now didn't exist back then. There definitely wasn't a Whole Foods or an Apple store, a Starbucks or a Dunkin' Donuts. It was local bars, local stores, and local people—and I really, really loved it.

What about restaurants?

Ramírez: Marlow & Sons and Diner were there before I moved here, along with other local restaurants too. Brooklyn cuisine replicated those neighborhood places. But my view on restaurants has changed. As a cook back then, I took home probably $475 a week, so going to restaurants was not necessarily something I could afford. The OG coffee shop Oslo was the only one in the neighborhood, or at least that I know of. There wasn't anything like Blue Bottle or Toby's yet.

Were you born in New York?

Ramírez: No, I was born and raised in Puerto Rico. I moved to the States the month that I turned 18 to go to culinary school in Vermont at the New England Culinary Institute. It was literally 89 degrees in San Juan and then when I moved to Vermont, it was ten below zero. The first two days were like, "Ooh, snow," and then every day after that it was, "Shit, this sucks." From there I moved to New Orleans for six months, then back to Vermont, then to Boston for a year, then Puerto Rico, and finally New York.

What about you Pam?

Pamela Yung: I was born in Cincinnati, Ohio, but I moved around a lot growing up. I lived in Cincinnati until I was 13, when we moved to Erie, Pennsylvania and eventually upstate New York. I went to school at the University of Michigan and, actually, I was not involved in food at all other than eating it.

When did food come into the picture for you?

Yung: I always had an interest in food, but I mostly just ate it. I baked a lot as a kid, but mostly just really simple stuff like cookies and muffins. In college, I started working side jobs in cafes, and after I graduated, I took a job at a design firm in Detroit—but I spent all of my spare time reading cookbooks. I'd literally take out 30 cookbooks from the library and just stay up all night reading them. I began making bread and ice cream from those recipes. I was obsessed. So I started moonlighting at a bakery while I was working at my other job. I would go two or three days a week at 3 a.m. to this bakery and then right after that, go straight to work.

Fortuitously, around the same time, I stumbled upon the website eGullet. It was a really nerdy forum for home cooks, as well as professional cooks and chefs, and I would read it religiously. One day, they had this feature on a chef named Will Goldfarb. In the interview, he said he was going to open a dessert bar in New York City, and he was looking for an apprentice. I was intrigued, so I wrote him an email. I really had no idea what I was getting into; I had no experience in the kitchen.

What happened?

Yung: Somehow, he responded: "Great, when can you come in for an interview?" I was going to New York City for Thanksgiving because my grandparents lived in Chinatown. I remember he showed me books from Pierre Gagnaire, and I just thought, "What is this?" I got so excited about the idea of this stuff in front me and so at the end of the day, he was like, "Okay, are you in? Shake my hand right now." I hadn't told anybody about it yet—not even my parents—but I shook his hand. I just knew I had to do it.

What did your parents say when you finally told them?

Yung: I waited until the morning before my flight to tell my parents. I sat them down and said, "Listen, I'm quitting my job. I'm moving to New York. I'm going to be an apprentice for this chef." It completely took them by surprise, but they had to take me to the airport so they couldn't really do anything about it. I got an email later that day from my parents, "This is really irresponsible. You have no idea what you're doing with your life. You're making horrible decisions. Why would you quit your job?" It was a very typical Asian parent thing. Already, doing design was a huge no-no for them; they really wanted me to be a doctor, lawyer, or computer scientist. So, just when they were getting used to me doing design, I tell them I'm going to work in a kitchen almost for free. They freaked out, and kept writing me these emails for years and years. We had a very bad relationship for a long time, because for them, they would say, "We didn't come to this country for you to work with your hands."

How did you deal with that?

Yung: I fought with them for a long time, but ultimately just ignored what they said. I gave my notice at the design firm, packed up, and I drove to New York with all of my stuff in early January of 2006.

Did you have an apartment?

Yung: My sister was living in New Jersey, so I was staying on her couch. I dropped off my stuff and went to my first day of work the next morning. I had no idea what I was getting myself into. I didn't even have knives. I just walked in. It was really crazy in retrospect. But it was probably a good thing; I never would have done it had I known what I was getting into.

How did you two meet?

Yung: We actually met at my birthday party. Momofuku Ssäm Bar had just opened. We were friends with Dave Chang, and I would hang out there a lot. I remember Dave showing me the business plan before he opened the place. I really wanted bo ssäm for my birthday, and the crew there invited a bunch of their friends and a lot of my other chef friends. Jose was working there at the time, so Dave brought him along with a couple of other cooks. That's where we first met, but we didn't really talk a lot.

Back then there was a really tight group. Maybe it still exists, but back then the downtown Manhattan restaurant crew was super tight. I remember the WD-50 guys hanging with the Room Four Dessert, Degustation, and Sandbar people. We all hung out at the same places.

Basically, all my friends were people that were working for Johnny Iuzzini, Sam Mason, and all of those pastry chefs. We would all hang out and go out, and that was the community. Although we worked really hard, it was really fun. It was like a party everyday. You would be interacting with all of these industry people and talking to guests, meeting people from all over the world. I was thrown into this sort of avant-garde pastry world but I really didn't know anything.

Do you think that this kind of tight knit community, where cooks all hang out together, is different today?

Yung: Well, we're older now. We're business owners, so we're not going out. I feel like there are still the 22-year-olds that have friends in all the cool restaurants. I think there's still some of that, but I don't know if it's the same. I feel like it was a lot more exciting to be a cook back then, to be honest.

Why?

Yung: I think that cook culture has changed a lot over the last ten years, and you're getting a different kind of person in the kitchen. Back then, we all had this common goal where we were all really shooting really high, working our asses off but also having fun. I guess I can't really speak for the younger generation, but I don't really see that as much in terms of that kind of drive—coming together to talk about your ideals and your plans.

But it's also different because a lot of the people we hung out with are now pretty successful. Like Rosio [Sánchez, former pastry chef at Noma and chef-owner of Hija de Sánchez in Copenhagen] started at Room Four Dessert and WD-50, so we became friends from the day that she moved here pretty much. I lived a block from WD-50 so we often would go out together, and then she would sleep over at my house because she lived in Harlem. People always joked, "Oh, you're at Pam's house. You should come in wearing the same clothing the next day," and she told me they would give her shit. But it really felt like a community.

What do you think the biggest differences now are?

Ramírez: When I moved here, I had a stage at Jean-Georges and another at Cru. The chef de cuisine at Jean-Georges said, "Get in contact with me within three days if you want the job." Then the guy from Cru called me to tell me I didn't get the job. So I called the Jean-Georges guy on the fourth day and he told me, "No, man. You didn't call me in three days, so you don't have the job." That's not how it works nowadays. I'm friends with the executive sous chef at Per Se, and they're hiring people straight out of culinary school with no experience. They're hiring people out of the military. When I was there, they were handpicking people out of the haystack.

You two worked at Roberta's as well, right?

Ramírez: I remember seeing Carlo [Mirarchi of Roberta's and Blanca] making a polenta with a poached egg and being like, "Who is this guy?" We volunteered to help out. It was completely different from what we knew; it was just wild, like anything goes—just chaotic.

Good chaotic?

Yung: Back then, it really appealed to me, because it felt like anything could happen. You could do whatever you wanted. It felt really homegrown. I had always been interested in bread, but I had never pursued it because the pay and lifestyle at bakeries in New York were horrible. So I said, "Hey, Carlo, I want to learn how to bake bread. Can I join as a baker working here part time?" And he said, "Actually, we really need a pastry chef. Do you think you could just make some desserts, and then you could do bread on the side?" At the time, my bank account just kept getting smaller and smaller every single day and I was like, "Okay, I need to take any job," so I started the next day.

What was that like?

Yung: When I started, they had nothing. They didn't have an ice cream maker. I had to start from zero and beg for equipment. They had this contraption that required an hour to make a quart of ice cream. It was 100 degrees in the kitchen, and the freezer didn't work properly. Nothing worked. Every day there was a disaster. Carlo really believed in me for some reason, and he supported everything I did. I worked by myself in the morning when no one was there, so no one was around to edit anything I did. But then I never was around for service. I never knew what the feedback was. I had total control and creative freedom. It was cool but it was also crazy.

How did you guys get started on your own restaurant?

Ramírez: We both worked at Isa and everyone got fired. We had invested so much in that place, and all of a sudden, we didn't have jobs. We didn't want to commit to someone else again, so we tried to see what we could do. A friend of ours owned a coffee shop called Whirlybird and he suggested that we cook there. So we started with that; it was very casual.

The space limitations dictated the style of cooking we were doing. We had to prepare everything at our apartment and bring it there—the plates, glassware, dishware, pots, and pans. It had to be food that we could travel with but would still be beautiful. There wasn't a lot of storage, so cooking meat on two induction burners was challenging.

Those early limitations dictated the direction of the cuisine, the level of refinement—or at least what refinement means to us, which is flavor and creativity, not necessarily taking tweezers to the food or whatever.

How would you characterize the food at Semilla?

Ramírez: We're focused on the product, and try to be in close proximity with the places where the product was procured. There is an emphasis on vegetables. I lived on a farm for six months where they had their own vegetable garden, animals, etcetera, and my intention was to recall that.

Why did you guys decide to focus on vegetables at Semilla?

Yung: When I was younger, I used to have no problem doing exhaustive tasting menus and eating late night food every single night. Now, in order to continue working the hours we work, we need to take better care of ourselves and eat better. I've become a lot more focused on what I'm eating and the quality of it. We put so much effort into what we eat and what we serve other people. So I've been learning how to work with different kinds of sugars and flours; it's really changed my approach to food. I don't think pastry needs to be completely over the top with cream, butter, and sugar. Actually, I really like to end on a refreshing note. I don't like to overwhelm people. It doesn't have to be a gut bomb at the end. I really have a hard time sitting through really heavy, long meat-centric meals, unless I'm specifically going somewhere for a steak. I want to feel like the food is fresh. I think that also eating around the world has changed the way I think about food in that way.

What do you mean by that?

Yung: We've become really close friends with a lot of farmers over the years, supporting them and really believing in what they do. We want to showcase their beautiful products and hard work. It's influenced the way we buy. And then when we learned more about the difficulties surrounding sustainable seafood, we wanted to feel like we were able to provide a really rich and satisfying meal without necessarily having a huge piece of protein. I think this way of eating—mostly vegetables—is the way more people will be eating in the future, as it becomes less sustainable to have meat three times a day. We both feel very strongly about that.

Ramírez: I come from a very political family. My dad was part of the separatist movement in Puerto Rico, and I grew up going to protests and all that. So for me, the way that we cook, to a certain extent, is a daily protest against the status quo for what the food systems in the United States are. It's a way of voicing my opinion without necessarily having to preach or go to protests or whatever.

How does that work in practice?

Ramírez: At Semilla, you will never find a piece of steak or a piece of fish because it's always about the vegetables. So we have scallops on the menu right now that come from Ireland. We're dealing with a fish buyer that goes to the port and delivers it to directly us rather than going through fish buyers who sell fish to a company here in New York that allows the fish to sit for another week before it gets delivered here. But in that dish, we're putting maybe half to three quarters of one tiny scallop that's getting marinated in rhubarb juice, which then endows the scallop with that super floral rhubarb flavor, and then we're topping it with a lot of green tomatoes and strawberries that are all marinated in strawberry vinegar.

The vegetable—in this case, rhubarb—is always the centerpiece.

When vegetarians come here with a partner who is not vegetarian, we serve both people an almost identical meal, except we just remove some protein aspects from the dish. Most of the time, they can't even tell the difference. I also think that vegetables, creatively speaking, are a whole lot more interesting than sirloin steak is.

Since it's a tasting menu, do you ever get customers who ask where the steak is?

Ramírez: In the beginning, when it was a little less clear, people were confused about exactly what vegetable-forward means, and we had some people write reviews saying, "We were waiting for the entree, and it never came" or "I was so disappointed that I had to get pizza afterwards." I think that now most people coming here are pretty familiar with what we're doing and open to it.

Would it be different if the restaurant were in Manhattan?

Ramírez: For a lot of people Brooklyn is a trek from Manhattan, so it's a conscious choice to come here. It's a destination, and you have to do a little bit of research. You're not just going to walk in from off the street. If we were to have just clientele off the street, we would be doing a lot more explaining in terms of, "Okay. This what to expect." Along those same lines, when we talk about vegetable-forward, we spent a month traveling through Vietnam a couple of years ago and cuisines like that, which have been around for a long time in a relatively poor country, rarely have a meal centered around a big piece of protein. Protein flavors the whole dish with fish sauce or ground pork, but it's not the centerpiece. Meat used to be something special. It wasn't something you could enjoy with every single meal. There were ways to get umami without a huge hunk of meat.

When you're creating a dish, where do you start?

Ramírez: Usually, you start with a meat then move to the starch then the vegetable and then the sauce. We do the exact same thing, but in reverse. So it's vegetable, starch, meat, then sauce.

Several other restaurants in Williamsburg refer to themselves as vegetable-driven with meat as a flavor enhancer. Why is this trend popping up here?

Ramírez: I hope I don't get murdered for saying this, but what people outside of New York now think of as Brooklyn cuisine is really just working directly with producers and cooking with those ingredients. It's that whole DIY idea: going to the farmers' market frequently and working with producers closely. I'm not saying that Manhattan restaurants don't go to the market. I'm saying that when you look at the restaurants that founded this style of cuisine—Roberta's, Vinegar Hill House, Andrew Tarlow's Diner and Marlow & Sons—they were working directly with farmers ten years ago before it was even cool. Eventually, because you're working with farmers, you end up cooking a certain way, and it changes who you are and what you're doing.

Do you have a favorite dish at Semilla?

Yung: Well, the only consistent thing is the bread, and that's been a huge passion for me. I really wanted to focus on different grains and different flavors in the bread. Before, I would always make the same bread with the same mix of flours. But here I've done a lot of experimenting: The bread here is different every single day. I keep thinking: What's my ideal bread? What does it feel like? Taste like? How would it support our local grain community? I'm still always like, "I can't believe I made that."

Corn Broth with Cuttle Fish, Wild Rice and Okra Blossoms

Recipe by José Ramírez-Ruiz from Semilla.

Cuttlefish

Marinate cuttlefish in white soy sauce for at least an hour.

Puffed Wild Rice

Heat canola oil in a large pot until temperature reaches 415°F.

Deep-fry 15 g wild rice at a time, removing grains from the oil with a spider or slotted spoon as soon the grains puff to avoid burning.

Place all puffed rice in a tray lined with paper towels and allow to drain. You may need to replace the towels several times to extract all excess oil.

Once the rice is fully drained and cooled, store in a tightly closed container lined with paper towels.

Dashi

Combine 1 liter of the water with kombu and simmer on low heat for 10 minutes.

Stir in bonito flakes and simmer for another 10 minutes.

Strain all solids through a fine-mesh sieve. Reserve liquid on the side.

Put all solids back into a pot and cover with the remaining 3 liters of water. Simmer on low heat for another 10 minutes.

Strain liquid and combine with the first extraction. Save the kombu and discard remaining solids.

Due to evaporation, you should end up with a little less than 4 liters of dashi broth total. Add water until you have 4 liters of dashi.

Pickled Kombu

Slice kombu into long, thin strips.

Combine vinegar, water, sugar, and salt. Bring to a simmer to dissolve all solids.

Add sliced kombu and simmer at low heat for 10 minutes.

Remove from heat and let the mixture cool to room temperature.

•••

CUTTLEFISH

170 g	cuttlefish, thinly sliced (sushi-grade, cleaned)
	white soy sauce (shoyu), to cover

PUFFED WILD RICE

1 L	canola oil
45 g	organic wild rice

DASHI

120 g	kombu
60 g	bonito flakes
4.5 L	filtered water

PICKLED KOMBU

	leftover kombu from making Dashi
470 ml	rice vinegar
470 ml	water
225 g	sugar
	salt (to taste)

Corn Broth with Cuttle Fish, Wild Rice and Okra Blossoms – *continuation*

Corn Kernels

Shuck one ear of corn, cut off ends of cob, and cut cob in half.

Using a small paring knife, carefully remove the kernels one at a time, keeping them intact.

Place all the kernels on a tray lined with parchment paper. Cover tightly with plastic wrap and steam at 212°F until the corn is cooked through, about 10 minutes.

Remove plastic wrap and allow to cool to room temperature.

Corn Broth

Shuck the ears of corn and, using a chef's knife, cut the kernels from the cob, saving the kernels to grind. Cut the shaved cobs into one-inch-thick slices.

In a pot, combine Dashi with the cut cobs, onion, garlic, and star anise. Cover with a lid and bring it to a simmer over low heat for about one hour.

Strain and discard solids.

Using the smallest dial of a meat grinder, grind the corn kernels.

Combine ground kernels and corn cob stock, and bring to a simmer, stirring constantly to avoid scorching.

Simmer until desired sweetness is achieved. Strain through a fine-mesh sieve and then again through a cheesecloth.

Season with salt and honey (Tabasco optional) and cool to room temperature.

Assembly

In a large mixing bowl, combine the cuttlefish, corn kernels, pickled kombu, and puffed wild rice. Toss together and divide among serving bowls.

Tear pieces of the okra (or squash) blossoms, and arrange them on top of the bowls as garnish.

Heat the corn broth and divide among the bowls, pouring it tableside.

—

CORN KERNELS

1 ear of corn

CORN BROTH

15 ears of corn

2 pods star anise

1 large Spanish onion, peeled and thinly sliced

5 cloves garlic, sliced

4 L dashi broth

salt

honey

Tabasco (optional)

#pamsbread
(sourdough with potatoes)

Recipe by Pam Yung from Semilla.

Bread and butter would be my last supper. The truth is, I'll likely spend my entire life trying to make a loaf that fulfills my wildest dreams. This is the thrill and agony I live with every day that I bake. My greatest joy is creating such a nuanced and expressive, yet humble food, using only the simplest of ingredients. Every time I get close, it feels like magic.

I first began baking with a wild levain [starter] at the Williamsburg restaurant Isa in 2012, and it changed everything for me. The investment I felt when I cared for that living being and observed its daily growth bred a certain intimacy with the dough. Although working with a levain is more demanding and time-consuming, the end product is well worth it. Good bread demands the best ingredients you can get your hands on. Spend time finding grain from a reputable and local grower or miller. This is the best way to guarantee that you will work with the most aromatic and responsive flour. Start simple, and then use your creativity to layer texture, flavor, and personality into your bread. I now call this recipe #pamsbread because, at this point, that's what everyone else calls it too.

LEVAIN

Starting a levain

Starting and maintaining a levain is an integral part of this process. If you don't already have one from a generous friend, you can start your own. Using your fingertips, mix the flours and water in a small container until no dry flour or big lumps remain. Cover with a towel, and let it ferment at room temperature for a few days until you start to see activity. It should puff up, bubble, and "rise" in volume.

Maintaining your levain

Prior to baking, make sure the levain is happily and regularly fed. If you don't bake regularly, it is okay to give your levain some time in the refrigerator. But, if you do so, take the levain out of the refrigerator at least 1 to 2 days prior to baking, and start it on a regular feeding schedule.

To feed culture, reserve 100 g of your levain and discard the rest. Replace the discarded portion with 100 g warm water and 100 g flour. Using your hands, mix to combine until no large lumps remain.

With regular feedings, you'll observe a pattern of rising and falling in your levain. It's prudent to take small tastes of your levain to understand how its flavor changes over time (young and sweet versus mature and sour).

Feed it twice daily—once in the morning and once in the evening—and at the same time each day. Marinate cuttlefish in white soy sauce for at least an hour.

•••

LEVAIN

STARTING A LEVAIN

75 g   whole wheat flour
75 g   bread flour
150 g warm water

MAINTAINING YOUR LEVAIN

100 g levain
100 g 50/50 flour
       (50 g whole wheat flour, 50 g bread flour)
100 g warm water

#pamsbread
(sourdough with potatoes) - *continuation*

BREAD RECIPE

Preparing the potatoes

Cook the potatoes with black peppercorns, thyme, and garlic at a slow simmer until tender.

Strain and remove aromatics.

Allow the potatoes to cool.

Using your fingertips, crush potatoes into dime-sized pieces.

Baking with your levain

In the morning, feed the levain and observe its activity. Within 2 to 3 hours, it's ready (this could vary depending on temperature). It should appear puffed and bubbly, and smell sweet and yeasty. To test whether the levain is ready to be used, drop a small piece into water—it should float.

Simultaneous to feeding the levain, mix flours and the first quantity of water (750 g) by hand, until no dry flour remains. Cover with a towel and let it rest. This is called the autolyse, and the starches and proteins in the flour begin to break down, helping to condition the dough for easier handling, stretchier dough, and hydration, ultimately yielding a better loaf.

When the levain is ripe, combine 200 g of it with the flour mixture, making sure to retain the remaining levain as your starter. (Do not discard remaining levain; you'll need this to refresh later in the evening.) Mix constantly, allowing the gluten to develop. It's critical to allow gluten formation before overwhelming the dough with the remaining water. The dough should begin to pull between your fingers, as opposed to looking soupy and wet. Then, slowly stream in the second batch of water, allowing it to fully absorb into the dough before adding more. Be patient. Stop periodically to allow the dough to rest and absorb the water before continuing. Finally, add the sea salt and mix until fully incorporated.

Place dough in a large bowl or square container that is large enough for the dough to grow. Cover with a loose lid or towel. Now, your dough will expand and ferment for about four to five hours at room temperature.

Every 30 minutes, you'll want to do some stretch-and-folds or "turns" to strengthen the gluten and create tension in the dough. To do so, wet your hands and reach under one side of the dough and fold it up and over to the opposite side. Repeat on the three other sides of the dough. Cover and let rest. Repeat this approximately every half hour.

Add-ins

You'll want to add salted potato pieces into the dough at about 1½ hours into the bulk fermentation process. Distribute the pieces evenly throughout the dough, doing a few "turns" with your hands to ensure that the pieces of potatoes don't cluster.

• • •

POTATOES

- 450 g potatoes (heirloom varieties, if possible)
- water, to cover
- 10 black peppercorns
- 5 sprigs thyme
- 4 cloves garlic, unpeeled
- salt, to season generously

BAKING WITH YOUR LEVAIN

- 100 g rye flour
- 100 g sprouted rye flour (if unavailable, substitute spelt, barley, or whole wheat flour)
- 200 g high-extraction wheat flour
- 600 g high-gluten wheat flour
- 750 g water
- 200 g ripe levain
- 100 g water
- 25 g sea salt

ADD-INS

- 450 g cooked and crushed potatoes, at room temperature

#pamsbread
(sourdough with potatoes) – *continuation*

Shaping

Once the dough has fermented sufficiently (the dough will increase in volume approximately 30% and appear shiny and lighter, and airier than when you began), it's time to shape.

Empty the dough onto a lightly floured work surface. Divide the dough into four equal rounds. Using a dough scraper in one hand, drag the dough in a circular motion along the work surface to create tension, guiding it with your less dominant hand. The dough should have a taut surface and look like a tight round.

After the dough has noticeably relaxed (approximately 20 to 40 minutes), begin to make the final shape. Prepare bread baskets by dusting them with a mixture of all-purpose and rice flour, in a 50/50 ratio. With the dough scraper in hand, flip the relaxed dough ball upside down onto the floured work surface. You want to create an even tighter ball. Grab each side of the dough, stretch it outwards, and fold each stretched piece toward the center, sealing opposite sides together. Continue doing so until the dough is noticeably tighter. With a dough scraper, transfer the dough into 9" bread baskets, seam side up. Let the dough rise at room temperature for 3-4 hours before baking.

If you don't want to bake right away, the bread baskets should be placed in the refrigerator for a slowed fermentation process for up to 12 hours.

Baking

If you don't have the luxury of a bread oven, you can make it work in your home oven with a few simple tools. A preheated Dutch oven or a cast iron pot will create a built-in steaming mechanism for the dough.

About 20 minutes before you are ready to bake, place cast-iron or Dutch oven with lid in the oven and preheat the oven to 500°F.

Once the oven has preheated, generously dust your cast-iron pan or Dutch oven with rice flour. Invert the loaf carefully into the preheated vessel, seam side down. Score the top of the dough with a sharp knife or razor. Cover with lid and put into the oven. Cooking time and temperature will vary from oven to oven, but I turn the temperature down to 480°F and bake for 20 minutes. After 20 minutes, uncover the pot to allow for the dough's remaining water to evaporate. Bake for an additional 20 to 25 minutes until it develops a dark golden, even reddish, hue and the loaf feels light and hollow.

Cool loaf on a rack.

Repeat as necessary for remaining loaves, ensuring the oven preheats sufficiently again before baking each loaf.

A loaf wrapped in plastic can last at room temperature for about a week. Alternatively, you can portion and freeze the finished loaf.

—

Peach Pit Custard

Recipe by Pam Yung from Semilla.

Saffron Agrodolce

Place glucose syrup, water, sugar, and vinegar (if amazake and white balsamic vinegars are unavailable, substitute high-quality white wine vinegar) into a small pot on low heat and simmer slowly, reducing until thickened. Remember that the mixture will thicken as it cools, so be careful not to over-reduce. Remove from the pot, stir in a pinch of saffron to taste, and set the pot in a warm place to let the saffron infuse. Season with salt.

Peach Pit (Noyaux) Custard

Place pits in a resealable plastic bag. On the floor (it's much easier than on a table), take a hammer to each stone to crack it open, revealing an "almond". Remove the almonds and set aside.

Bloom gelatin in ice water until gelatin is completely softened.

Heat heavy cream in a small saucepan. Dissolve sugar in cream. Scald the cream then remove from heat just before it boils. (You should see steam coming off of the surface of the cream, as if it's about to simmer.) In a blender, add all the peach pits and some of the heated cream. Blend on high speed (hold the lid down with a folded kitchen towel over the hole in the lid—blender tops can explode with hot liquid otherwise) until thoroughly processed. Add the mixture back into the pot of hot cream; cover and allow it to infuse, about 10 minutes. If sufficiently infused (strong, slightly bitter almond flavor), remove cover and melt in previously bloomed gelatin.

Cool custard by pouring it into a small metal bowl set over a large one filled with an ice bath. Stir the custard with a spatula as it cools to prevent the gelatin from hardening around the edges.

Divide among 6 oz. ramekins (about 70 g custard per ramekin). Place in refrigerator to set, about 2 hours.

•••

SAFFRON AGRODOCLE

- 400 g glucose syrup
- 200 g water
- 75 g sugar
- 100 g amazake vinegar
- 100 g white balsamic vinegar
- salt
- saffron

PEACH PIT (NOYAUX) CUSTARD

- 1 L heavy cream
- 50 g sugar
- 8 peach pits (or the pits of any available stone fruits), with peach flesh reserved for slicing
- 8 g sheet gelatin (silver)

Peach Pit Custard – *continuation*

Almond Milk

Soak almonds in water overnight. The following day, blend thoroughly then pass through a fine nut milk bag.

Almond Milk Foam

Season almond milk lightly with some sugar and salt. Using a hand blender on low speed and angled slightly outside of the liquid (the blade should be partially submerged to allow aeration of the liquid and form bubbles), blend in lecithin, approximately 1/8 tsp. at a time, until the froth holds a medium-sized bubble. Reserve in refrigerator until cold.

Peaches

If the peaches are ripe, there is no need to do anything to them. If not, they may need a little bit of sugar after slicing.

To assemble

Remove custard from the refrigerator. Slice peaches thinly on mandolin. Arrange them on top of the custard by curling them against each other. Sauce generously with the saffron agrodolce. Using a hand blender, foam the almond milk and spoon over the peaches. Serve immediately.

—

ALMOND MILK

250 g	Noto brand almonds (online from Gustiamo)
1 L	cold water

ALMOND MILK FOAM

1 L	almond milk
50 g	confectioner's sugar
5 g	salt
1 g	lecithin

PEACHES

1	Depending on size, approximately 1 peach per serving

Claus Meyer

MEYERS BAGERI, WILLIAMSBURG
40.71436° N, 73.95896° W

Claus Meyer was one of the founding fathers of Noma, the Copenhagen restaurant that launched the new Nordic movement and, by extension, the international obsession with hyperlocal, hyper-seasonal ingredients that has dominated restaurant kitchens for the better part of the last decade. Meyer, now a successful restaurateur in Denmark, recently shifted his focus to New York instead. This year, he opened the Great Northern Food Hall, a 5,000-square-foot market in Grand Central Terminal devoted to Scandinavian food and education; Agern, a restaurant in that same terminal; and Meyers Bageri, a Danish bakery in Williamsburg. But in a city where it is notoriously difficult for restaurateurs to open up shop—especially foreign restaurateurs—his restaurants, including Meyers Bageri, have already seamlessly integrated. Here, Meyer reveals a foreign perspective on eating in Brooklyn, and sheds light on the importance of local, sustainable grains for the community and the environment.

Why did you decide to open a bakery in New York?

I wanted to make sure bakeries would be a part of the operation, because my goal is to bring the best of what I've learned from what we've done in Denmark to America. We have a strong grain legacy. We are a bread nation. When my friends and I started the Nordic food movement and restaurant Noma, we were thinking about the untapped potential of bread. We decided to think about bread the same way we thought about everything else: with the notion of terroir, so that bread could reflect a place. We wanted grain that is unique to our geography and history. We wanted to explore the interface between what's delicious and what's healthy.

What do you mean by that?

If you look at Wonderbread in America, it's made from high-yield modern wheat, and after all of the additives and sugar, it's very far from being an authentic food item. Ideally, we'd be eating 100% whole grain, but if you do that, then bread would be like eating cabbage all day long, and nobody wants to do that. What we want is the softness and moisture in bread, but we don't want it to be overly chewy or gooey.

What are the barriers to making that happen?

When we first started making bread, we actually asked ourselves, why in the world are people making bread with flour that isn't organic? The cost of the flour in the bread is so little. The cost is rent, manpower, the space, and the equipment. It makes sense to use better flour once you know that, for every single kilo of organic flour you use, 330 liters of groundwater per week will be freed from the risks of pesticides. There's so much at stake. The impact of grain production on the environment is so tremendous. It's important to get bread right, and democratize that kind of bread to as many people as possible. We need to change bread together—build wonderful recipes and share them with people.

I didn't come here to teach Americans how to make bagels. We're spreading something that means something to us, whether it's Danishes or sustainable bread from locally grown flour.

What differences, if any, are there between your locations in Manhattan and Brooklyn?

We insisted on building a bakery in Grand Central Terminal so that bread could be baked fresh onsite all day long. We mix the dough for Grand Central in Queens and then bring the dough to the bakery. There, we also have passionate craftsmen running around, talking to guests and the front-of-house team.

In Williamsburg, we do everything onsite. We don't have deliveries from trucks at odd hours. We grind all of the flour ourselves. There's just more space.

How did you find the Williamsburg space?

I love where we are on Driggs Ave in Williamsburg. New places are always opening there; it's growing. It was just a spontaneous decision. There aren't very many spaces that lend themselves to real bakeries either. And people who live in Brooklyn are more willing to walk or ride a bicycle a short distance to get something extraordinary. We bake three times a day.

You have a very international perspective. What is Brooklyn food culture, in your opinion?

I can't say I'm an authority on that issue yet but, in general, from what I've experienced, it's the most dynamic and expressive place in the food world, and

in the world of crafts. There have been so many interesting micro-manufacturers, specialized retail shops, and wonderful restaurants of all kinds that have started out there. Copenhagen is dynamic, but not like Brooklyn.

Has there been anything about opening in New York that has surprised you?

People here do not buy as many whole loafs as they do in Denmark. So we had to recalibrate the number of big breads we made compared to the number of small, filled buns. As our breads get more traction, more people will want to buy whole loaves. Even the rye bread is winning fans, and that's 100% whole grain bread with no fat and no added sugar.

I think that the city has been more inviting and has embraced us in a way I didn't expect. On the other hand, we really have to fight to change the way people walk and experience our restaurants and bakeries. In Manhattan, people walk on 42nd Street and don't know we exist. We're like, by the way, there's a food hall in here. It requires a lot of hard work to inspire someone to walk 20 meters to us.

How do you do it then?

New guests come by and some people come in for happy hour at the bar at Agern then realize we're open for breakfast. It's a lot of word of mouth. We don't have the budget to advertise.

How would you locate New York's food scene in the context of the rest of the world's?

Somehow it feels like the epicenter of the world of food, and even the world as such. The best journalists and new trends start here. Some of the best people in the food industry work, or have worked, in this city. It's the most competitive place in the world to open a business by far. It's maybe elitist too.

But Manhattan and Brooklyn are very different. If you see something brand new that the world has never seen before, it probably started in Bushwick. Brooklyn has lower rents so you can afford to take bigger chances. In that way, it has a much more innovative, daring, and creative food scene than Manhattan, where most people expect a certain experience. It's just a different clientele. In Brooklyn, anything is possible—even a restaurant housed in a couple of shipping containers with a grill outside.

My Chinatown
By Clare Mao

To grow up Chinese in an American city means the geographic center of your universe is your local chinatown. Everything radiates from there. I grew up in Queens, so my universe unfolded itself outward from Flushing. I had obliquely heard of Manhattan's Chinatown, probably in the same way people elsewhere in the country hear about New York City. And I vaguely knew Chinese people lived in Brooklyn, because my parents did when they first immigrated here, before they settled in Queens. But it wasn't until I was in college, living among the cornfields of Iowa that I first learned of Brooklyn's Chinatown, located along Eighth Avenue in Sunset Park.

In college, I gravitated with an annoying inevitability toward the other New Yorkers on campus to participate in the insufferable regional superiority in which we specialize. It would take the trauma of being over a thousand miles from home, living in middle America, for me to transcend my innate distrust of the other boroughs. When I left home for Iowa, I considered myself open-minded. But I still took it for granted that I would be able to buy star anise and century eggs at any grocery store. I assumed that most of my classmates would understand not only the semantic but also the cultural and mouthfeel difference between hand-pulled and knife-cut noodles. I soon learned that I was wrong. From Iowa, where I arrived in 2010, the closest chinatown, the way I understood it, was four hours and a state away.

In New York, a city of excess, three of the five boroughs have chinatowns. Manhattan's Chinatown is the original capital-C Chinatown, just as New York City is often shorthand for Manhattan, while the other boroughs still need specification. Flushing, where I grew up, is technically a Chinatown in that it is a neighborhood in which many Chinese immigrants have settled and make a living. Brooklyn's Chinatown is the newest of the three.

My parents moved to Flushing after they first immigrated here for a number of reasons, chief among them that Flushing is largely populated by immigrants from Taiwan and urban Chinese areas, where Mandarin Chinese is spoken. Queens, which is much more suburban and spatially generous than Manhattan, holds an understandable appeal for immigrants like my parents, who are college-educated and city-grown, who aspired to professional careers beyond the restaurants they both worked in upon their arrival to the United States. Flushing represented opportunity and social mobility—a fresh start with the comforts of home.

I moved back to Flushing immediately after graduation and vowed never to take the ease of buying Taiwanese popcorn chicken, hot oil wontons, guava candy, and fish heads for granted ever again. A year and a half later, I moved out of my high school bedroom into an apartment in South Brooklyn. What I worried about most wasn't not paying bills or roommate compatibility—it was where I was supposed to go for groceries. At 22 years old, I realized I didn't know how to shop for food anywhere that is not an Asian grocery store.

Local grocery stores in Flatbush were enough to sustain me for the first few weeks, just until the Tupperware of rice I brought from home ran out. While most grocery stores stock jasmine or minute rice, my holy grail of rices is Kokuho medium-grain rice, sold almost exclusively in Asian supermarkets. I needed to get my hands on it.

I remembered my classmates' enthusiasm for Brooklyn's Chinatown, which turns out to be kissing cousins with Flatbush. The two neighborhoods are conveniently connected by the B35 bus. When I arrived for the first time, in search of Kokuho, I found that Brooklyn's Chinatown presented itself in a straight line along Eighth Avenue in Sunset Park, unlike the pinwheel arrangement of the streets of Manhattan's Chinatown or the perpendicular main streets of Flushing. I am always shocked when other people's chinatowns don't look like mine.

The B35 drops you off at the northernmost end of Eighth Avenue. There are a few restaurants, laundromats, and karaoke bars at that end, but it's quiet

for the most part. Brooklyn's Chinatown occupies only one stretch of Sunset Park. The majority of Sunset Park houses a Hispanic population so significant, the food appeases even the snobbiest of Southern California expats.

The further south you walk, the closer you get to storefronts stacked on top of other storefronts, steps that lead to basement massage parlors, food carts, and stores with wide-open doors, where merchandise ranging from brooms to slippers and slightly defective plastic toys spill outside. It culminates on 65th Street at East Harbor Seafood Palace, where a dim sum restaurant and banquet hall stands regally among a string of car garages.

Overwhelmed by that first trip, I limited myself to two stops: Thanh Da II for bánh mì and Vietnamese coffee, and Fei Long Market for groceries, the most important of which was a 15-pound bag of my beloved rice.

My euphoria at having found the fraternal twin of my favorite Flushing grocery store meant I ended up with bags of snacks, vegetables, raw meat, and fruits that, combined, weigh at least 15 pounds more. The journey of carrying these groceries home made my arms shake. When I did finally make it home, I rewarded myself with the bánh mì. Though it spent a good two hours trapped in its own dampness in a paper bag, I remember how the bread was still sharp enough to cut the roof of my mouth, soothed only by the tang of pickled radish and the sugar of barbecued pork. It remains the best bánh mì I have ever had.

These days, when I talk about Sunset Park, I am prone to embarrassing, enthusiastic hyperbole. There's Yun Nan Flavor Garden, where the star dish is the guoqiao ("crossing the bridge") noodles. Rumor has it that the dish was born when the wife of a scholar studying for his imperial exams on a small island discovered that her noodles became cold and soggy by the time she crossed the bridge to feed her studious husband. She had the ingenious idea of separating the broth, noodles, and ingredients, only mixing them once she had crossed the bridge. In the restaurant, it's not as long of a walk from the kitchen to one of the restaurant's five tables, but the performance is part of the appeal. There's nothing I love more than a dispassionate waitress setting in front of me a plate of raw, sliced meat, a dish containing a single egg yolk, a bowl of noodles, and a basin-sized bucket of white pepper broth. I savor the sight for a second, not even long enough to take a photo for Instagram, before sliding everything into the bowl of broth. It's too big for a single person, but not big enough for two to share.

There's also Fei Long Market, where the vegetables remain inexplicably crisp a week and a half after purchase, the Dorian Grays of the produce world. There's Mister Hotpot, which I refused to believe was the best hotpot in the city until, of course, I tried it for myself. And there's East Harbor Seafood Palace, my favorite dim sum in New York. When I was younger, dim sum was a Saturday morning treat, often an olive branch extended after nasty fights with my mom; there's a Pavlovian comfort even now, where it's my hangover brunch of choice.

Part of my enthusiasm for Brooklyn's Chinatown, in lieu of my own, is magnified by the knowledge of my mom's recent move to Staten Island, physically separating the emotional center of my universe from its location. The shuttle bus ride from Brooklyn's Chinatown to Flushing takes about an hour, and public transportation takes even longer. It's just inconvenient enough that nowadays I visit Flushing about as often as I did when I was in Iowa. No Chinatown will ever be quite as good as your Chinatown. But in the absence of mine, I'll always have Sunset Park.

addresses and coordinates

Achilles Heel
180 West St
Brooklyn, NY 11222
40.73317° N, 73.95956° W

Anthony & Son Panini Shoppe
433 Graham Ave.
Brooklyn, NY 11211
40.71791°N, 73.94529°W

Bamonte's
32 Withers St
Brooklyn, NY 11211
40.71656° N, 73.95117° W

Ben's Best
96-40 Queens Blvd
Rego Park, NY 11374
40.72937° N, 73.86137° W

Blanca / Roberta's
261 Moore St
Brooklyn, NY 11206
40.70507° N, 73.93359° W

Brooklyn Farmacy & Soda Fountain
513 Henry St
Brooklyn, NY 11231
40.68401° N, 73.99931° W

Brooklyn's Natural
49 Bogart St #1
Brooklyn, NY 11206
40.70528°N, 73.93329°W

Cacao Prieto
218 Conover St
Brooklyn, NY 11231
40.67731° N, 74.01531° W

Chef's Table at Brooklyn Fare
200 Schermerhorn St
Brooklyn, NY 11201
40.68864° N, 73.98589° W

Contra
138 Orchard St
New York, NY 10002
40.71990° N, 73.98915° W

Crown Fried Chicken
1263 Nostrand Ave.
Brooklyn, NY 11226
40.65617°N, 73.94994°W

Diner
85 Broadway,
Brooklyn, NY 11249
40.71071° N, 73.96555° W

East Harbor Seafood Palace
714 65th St
Brooklyn, NY 11220
40.63353° N, 74.01434° W

Emmy Squared
364 Grand St
Brooklyn, NY 11211
40.71230°N, 73.9556°W

Faro
436 Jefferson St
Brooklyn, NY 11237
40.70742° N, 73.92284° W

Fei Long Market
4423 8th Ave
Brooklyn, NY 11220
40.64386° N, 74.00050° W

Five Leaves
18 Bedford Ave
Brooklyn, NY 11222
40.72372° N, 73.95162° W

Glady's
788 Franklin Ave.
Brooklyn, NY 11238
40.67171°N, 73.95788°W

Gloria's
764 Nostrand Ave
Brooklyn, NY 11216
40.67241° N, 73.95051° W

Grimaldi's Pizza
1 Front St.
Brooklyn, NY 11201
40.70264°N, 73.99323°W

Hops & Hocks
2 Morgan Ave.
Brooklyn, NY 11237
40.70412°N, 73.93117°W

Ikea
1 Beard St.
Brooklyn, NY 11231
40.67197°N, 74.01146°W

Jack From Brooklyn
177 Dwight St.
Brooklyn, NY 11231
40.67364°N, 74.01150°W

Jay & Lloyd's Kosher Deli
2718 Avenue U
Brooklyn, NY 11229
40.59998° N, 73.94410° W

Junior's Cheesecake
386 Flatbush Ave Ext.
Brooklyn, NY 11201
40.69017°N, 73.98194°W

Katz's Delicatessen
205 E Houston St
New York, NY 10002
40.72227° N, 73.98748° W

Kings County Distillery
299 Sands St
Brooklyn, NY 11205
40.69948° N, 73.97864° E

L&B Spumoni Gardens
2725 86th St
Brooklyn, NY 11223
40.59471° N, 73.98131° W

Lilia
567 Union Ave
Brooklyn, NY 11222
40.71738° N, 73.95218° W

Lucali
575 Henry St
Brooklyn, NY 11231
40.68180° N, 74.00029° W

Maison Premiere
298 Bedford Ave
Brooklyn, NY 11211
40.71425° N, 10.14834° W

Marlow & Daughters
95 Broadway
Brooklyn, NY 11211
40.71057° N, 73.96508° W

Marlow & Sons
81 Broadway
Brooklyn, NY 11249
40.71066° N, 73.96569° W

Mast Brothers
111 N 3rd St
Brooklyn, NY 11211
40.71673° N, 73.96160° W

Meyers Bageri
667 Driggs Ave
Brooklyn, NY 11211
40.71436° N, 73.95896° W

Mister Hotpot
5306 8th Ave
Brooklyn, NY 11220
40.63938° N, 74.00587 ° W

Nathan's Famous
1310 Surf Ave
Brooklyn, NY 11224
40.57527° N, 73.98146° W

New York Distilling Company
79 Richardson St
Brooklyn, NY 11211
40.71848° N, 73.94876° W

Okonomi / Yuji Ramen
150 Ainslie St
Brooklyn, NY 11211
40.71253° N, 73.94878° W

Osakana
290 Graham Ave
Brooklyn, NY 11211
40.71224° N, 73.94375° W

Peter Pan Donut
727 Manhattan Ave
Brooklyn, NY 11222
40.72608° N, 73.95230° W

Pizza Moto
338 Hamilton Ave.
Brooklyn, NY 11231
40.67444°N, 74.00072°W

Pok Pok
117 Columbia St
Brooklyn, NY 11231
40.68758° N, 74.00122° W

Reynard
80 Wythe Ave
Brooklyn, NY 11249
40.72188° N, 73.95809° W

Sarge's
548 3rd Ave
New York, NY 10016
40.74735° N, 73.97724° W

Semilla
No. 5, 160 Havemeyer St
Brooklyn, NY 11211
40.71145° N, 73.95785° W

Shalom Japan
310 S 4th St
Brooklyn, NY 11211
40.70915° N, 73.95579° W

Spritzenhaus33
33 Nassau Ave
Brooklyn, NY 11222
40.72336° N, 73.95283° W

Thanh Da II
6008 7th Ave.
Brooklyn, NY 11220
40.63663°N, 74.01219°W

The Four Horsmen
295 Grand St
Brooklyn, NY 11211
40.71308° N, 73.95733° W

The Odeon
145 W Broadway
New York, NY 10013
40.71697° N, 74.00783° W

Tom's Diner
782 Washington Ave
Brooklyn, NY 11238
40.67447° N, 73.96341° W

Tørst / Luksus
615 Manhattan Ave
Brooklyn, NY 11222
40.67447° N, 73.95077° W

Totonno's
1524 Neptune Ave
Brooklyn, NY 11224
40.57882° N, 73.98380° W

Vinegar Hill House
72 Hudson Ave.
Brooklyn, NY 11201
40.70275°N, 73.98128°W

Wildair
142 Orchard St
New York, NY 10002
40.72002° N, 73.98916° W

Wyhte Hotel
80 Wythe Ave
Brooklyn, NY 11249
40.72188° N, 73.95809° W

Yun Nan Flavor Garden
5121 8th Ave.
Brooklyn, NY 11220
40.64000°N, 74.00458°W